David Williams

Lessons to a Young Prince

Third Edition

David Williams

Lessons to a Young Prince
Third Edition

ISBN/EAN: 9783337164782

Printed in Europe, USA, Canada, Australia, Japan

Cover: Foto ©ninafisch / pixelio.de

More available books at **www.hansebooks.com**

LESSONS

TO A

YOUNG PRINCE.

GEORGE PRINCE of WALES.

Published as the Act directs, Sep.r 17.t 1790.

LESSONS
TO A
YOUNG PRINCE,
BY AN
𝔒𝔩𝔡 𝔖𝔱𝔞𝔱𝔢𝔰𝔪𝔞𝔫,
ON THE
PRESENT DISPOSITION IN EUROPE
TO A
GENERAL REVOLUTION.

THE THIRD EDITION.

With the Addition of a Lesson on the
MODE OF STUDYING AND PROFITING
By Reflections on the
FRENCH REVOLUTION,
BY THE RIGHT HONOURABLE
EDMUND BURKE.

Quod munus reipublicæ afferre majus meliusque possumus, quam si docemus atque erudimus juventutem his præsertim moribus atque temporibus, quibus ita prolapsa est, ut omnium opibus refrænanda atque coercenda sit.   Cic. de Div. lib. ii. ver. 4.

LONDON:
PRINTED FOR H. D. SIMMONS, PATER-NOSTER ROW.
M.DCC.XC.

INTRODUCTION.

Every Writer wishes to have something understood, though he may seldom suggest the truth, respecting himself.

That I am approaching the extremity of life, may be credited, from my garrulity, from a general recurrence to distant events, as authorities, and from an affectation of prophecy or prediction.

—That I am disinterested, will not be supposed, at a time when the possibility of disinterestedness is disputed. Concealing my name,

even

even from the Printer and Publisher; laying indiscriminately before the exalted Personage I address, the truths that occur to me; and censuring equally his friends and opponents: it will be difficult, for it is difficult to myself, to imagine any interests actuating my mind, besides those of a public nature.

That I have not been a spectator only of the incidents of this age, every man of business will discern by internal evidence—That I am not an Author by profession, will be perceived by the lowest retainer of periodical criticism—My great object is, to rouse latent principles in a mind I think excellent, which has been neglected, or misled with design. If I succeed, I shall silently carry the satisfaction to the tomb that awaits me—If I fail, my last; will only share the fate of some former efforts—and their inefficacy will reconcile me to their oblivion.

CONTENTS.

LESSON I.
VIEW of the Prince's Education, and its Effects, — Page 1

LESSON II.
The Subject continued, — 11

LESSON III.
The Principles of Society, — 20

LESSON IV.
Constitution of England, — 25

LESSON V.
The Subject continued, — 39

LESSON VI.
Speculations, — 49

CONTENTS.

LESSON VII.
The American Revolution, - - - - - - - - - 58

LESSON VIII.
Constitution of France, - - - - - - - - - - 71

LESSON IX.
Principles of Legislation, - - - - - - - - - 92

LESSON X.
Mode of studying and profiting by Mr. Burke's Reflections on the late Revolution in France, ... 100

LESSONS

TO

A YOUNG PRINCE.

LESSON I.

VIEW OF THE PRINCE'S EDUCATION, AND ITS EFFECTS.

Privatas spes agitantes, sine publica cura. Tac.

DEMETRIUS Phalereus advised Ptolomy to study books; because things might be written in them, which his friends dared not advise.

Your Royal Highness is respectfully requested to consider the present section as an historical picture, in which you are the principal figure.

It is the reproach of the English education, that ornamental objects are preferred to those of utility; and an invariable mode of forming a scholar is applied to all the purposes of life. The preceptors of your Royal Highness are not answerable for the defects of a plan, in the formation of which they were not consulted.* They may be sufficiently justified by your proficiency in the belles lettres, and in the general accomplishments of a gentleman.

In moral arrangements, and in prudential preparations for the first impressions of society, the royal system was extremely defective. The education of the King had been monastic; and the Queen, bred in the œconomy of a little court, introduced a species of penury, as unfavourable to the minds, as it may be advantageous to the private fortunes of the royal children.

The moment of your Royal Highness's emancipation was that of a prisoner from confinement: you

---

* The question, 'Whether it was expedient the Princes 'should be scholars?' greatly agitated the domestic cabinet of B—— House almost a year. Dr. M— and Mr. J— had engaged them in the road of knowledge. Lord H— traversed their endeavors; and they were exchanged for the supple H—d and the insignificant A—.

plunged

plunged into the joys of fociety, with the avidity of one who had never tafted joy.

The ftrong contraft formed by the pleafurable World and Buckingham-houfe: and the petty fpirit of reproach and crimination incident to parents of reclufe difpofitions—generated that oppofition, of which the great factions of the time availed themfelves, and to which alone it can be beneficial. It was tafte rather than judgment that determined your opinion on every thing foftered at Buckingham-houfe; and the maxims of that houfe, which precipitated you into the arms of party, will fhortly be difcerned to have no affinity with thofe of real prudence, or real wifdom

That I am not devoted to the party at Buckingham-houfe—for I call every combination *a party*, which is not formed on public principles—you will often in thefe lucubrations have occafion to perceive. The great evil of the oppofition that boafts your Royal Highnefs's fanction is, that by an odium which time and talents have not abated, it fhadows an adminiftration incapable, ignorant, and at enmity with the effential principles of a free conftitution. The prefent miniftry embrace every plaufible pretence to circumscribe and abolish the trial by jury; bestow honors and benefices with views of corrupt influence slightly disguised; employ the pretence of paying off the national debt, to increase taxes and multiply establishments for private purposes: and they involve the country in a predatory war, in hopes some chances may furnish pretences for checking the progress of that liberty, which at this time menaces the insidious chicane of the present extraordinary administration; which may call Britain as well as France to its standard; and bestow on its ministers the fate of Breteuil, Brienne, Launay, and Calonne. With this actual character, and with these known views, ministers are secure of their places, and may proceed without danger, in advancing the interests of their connections, and injuring those of the public; in insults to all rank, merit, and service, not submissive to their will: and in the most impudent jobs for parliamentary corruption—Why?—Not because they are protected by your Royal Father—not from their interest or connections in the country—not by their abilities and talents— BUT MERELY BY THE UNIVERSAL DREAD OF THE DEPREDATIONS OF A NEEDY AND PROFLIGATE CABAL.

CABAL. Let this dread be removed; let the people of England be convinced, that the confequence of difmiffing the prefent adminiftration *will not be* the introduction of this cabal into power, Pitt, and the corrupt clufter furrounding him, would inftantly fink under the weight of the public refentment of his perfidious fervility in all the mafqued and cowardly machinations of defpotifm.

Pitt, therefore, may thank your Royal Highnefs for the profpect of permanence in a fituation for which he has no better qualifications than any other loquacious barrifter, who, by the habit of cloathing profufely and indifcriminately the ideas of others, lofes the power of inventive conception, and becomes as deftitute of original ideas, as of real honour and moral principle.

Your Royal Highnefs will think me miftaken, becaufe you will not eafily imagine I have more wifdom or better information, than the perfons on whofe talents you rely.

" What!" your Royal Highnefs may fay, " fhall
" I attend to the opinions of an unknown writer,
" who may be a dotard, in oppofition to thofe of a
" Fox, a Burke, a Sheridan, whofe abilities are
" acknow-

" acknowledged to be superlative, and who are forced from the public helm only by the malignity of fortune?"

That I am unknown, is in my favour. By announcing my name, I might put in a claim to the attention and patronage of your Royal Highness. That the abilities of the gentlemen you protect are brilliant and splendid, I will allow; but that they are superlative, or of the first order of human talents, I will examine; and if you will have the patience to attend me, I will enable your Royal Highness to judge.

On a slight recollection of the political atchievements of Fox, Burke, and Sheridan, your Royal Highness will perceive, that they often furnished high and rapturous entertainment for numerous and mingled audiences; and that on questions of great importance, and in situations of considerable difficulty, their abilities have always disappointed their friends.

I am going to hazard an opinion, on which I would hazard my life—that Mr. Fox, by far the superior man of the party, is remarkably defective in the great and inventive properties of wisdom—schemes,

schemes, plans, information, or materials, have ever been collected for Mr. Fox by all the talents and industry of a powerful party; and he has, above all men, the faculty of instantly giving order and expression to uncouth and enormous masses: but his mind not embracing the origin of measures, it is a chance that he directs them to the ruin or to the advantage of his party. I will give as instances—the coalition—the India bill—the inherent right to the regency—and the trial of Warren Hastings—events which mark the public life of Mr. Fox with national odium; and he has incurred it, not from dishonesty, for if there be an honest man among all the political adventurers and champions of the time, he is Charles Fox; but for want of abilities, for want of wisdom.—

Who projected the coalition, I am not informed. By internal evidence, I should adjudge it the idea of Burke: the extravagant absurdity of it suits no other mind.

The India bill, I am well assured, is Burke's own offspring; and it strongly bears the impression of its parent.

The doctrine of hereditary regency was furnished by Lord Loughborough (the well-known Wedderburne)

burne) with abundant promises of authorities and reasons, which were never fulfilled.

In the trial of Hastings, eloquence has been employed, like water in an inundation, without judgment and without advantage.

All the objects in the contemplation of Mr. Fox on these celebrated occasions, might have been obtained—not only without infamy, but with applause.

Mr. Pitt has obtained them all, with abilities greatly inferior, but with the art of profiting by the errors of Mr. Fox. He has all the advantages of the coalition, by detaching Robinson from his old master. He has acquired more power in India than Mr. Fox aimed at, by only saving appearances with the King. He has acquired popularity by a doctrine respecting the power of two estates in Parliament, which if advanced by Mr. Fox, would have procured his impeachment: and he has rendered his opponents the instruments of his own purposes respecting Mr. Hastings.*

* If the conduct of the Minister were thoroughly understood in this business; if the motives of his sudden conversion to the opinion that Hastings should be impeached, were stated to Parliament and the country by an able and honest senator, we might see what we have long wanted, a Minister rendered actually responsible.

Such are the *superlative* abilities of your Royal Highness's principal, though, perhaps, not your favorite counsellor.

That Burke has talents, no man of sense will deny: but they are superficial, ostentatious, and want the guidance of judgment and science. *Satis eloquentiæ sapientiæ parum.*

Sheridan, with equal imagination, has more art; and being educated in the Green Room of the Theatre, understands the method of giving effect to every sentiment, action, and expression. But he is a mere artificer of scenes: his orations are plays in a new form; and they produce amusement or admiration, never conviction or respect.

The abilities and accomplishments of the three united would not constitute a statesman, or a truly great man. Their fancies or imaginations are not balanced by science; by that high, exalted reason which is formed by the calm and patient study of philosophy, a profound acquaintance with history, and the strict discipline of mathematics.

Your Royal Highness will therefore derive no real advantage from the boasted talents of these orators, unless they should answer Rabelais' description

tion of Pantagruel, who covered his whole army with his tongue, and sheltered it from inclemencies and inconveniences.

LESSON

LESSON II.

THE SUBJECT CONTINUED.

Rebus minoribus quifque tendentes. Tac.

I KNOW your Royal Highnefs is not remarkable for long or patient attention; and that the important habit of it has not been an object in your education.

I have, therefore, divided the fubject of the firft leffon I mean to fubmit to your perufal.

If the champions of the party you have efpoufed are fuch as I have defcribed—if the combined talents of the phalanx have not produced public refpect— what can your Royal Highnefs hope from a fyftem of favouritifm for the elevation of the moft exceptionable.

I do not concur in the trivial objections to Mr. Sheridan's origin, education, and deftination— If thefe were more exceptionable than they are reprefented

fented to be; they are circumftances in which the will and character of the man are not concerned.

I do not object to any irregularities, which are the fair refult of youthful and ftrong paffions.

I believe not one half of the common catalogue of his ftratagems and expedients to procure or avoid the payment of money.

But Sheridan is a camelion: his words, his fentiments, his paffions, take their colour from furrounding objects: he feems every thing to every man; is unfufceptible of real attachment; and though he may have protectors and admirers, Sheridan is without a friend.

You may peculiarly diftinguifh fuch a man—you may, on fome future occafion, give him the lead in your councils: but the POWER OF A THRONE would not fuftain him in the fituation.

Recollect the manner in which propofitions from him have been received in Parliament, that would have covered another with glory. Recollect the principal caufe, in the obtrufion of his interference during the illnefs of your Royal Father, and in the method of managing your paffions to the purpofes of his ambition.

The

The artifices of that period were so clearly and instantaneously perceived, that the nation felt to its utmost extremities a repugnance and detestation, which the amiable character and manners of your Royal Highness could hardly restrain within the limits of peace.

Can your Royal Highness imagine, the country was agitated or interested by the question of right? Do you suppose, the probable accession of the respectable and patriotic families of Devonshire and Portland occasioned alarm? Or can your Royal Highness conceive, that exchanging Pitt for Fox in the offices of venality, could excite the general terror, which sanctioned resolutions of Parliament the most absurd, the most unconstitutional, the most inimical to Liberty; which embalmed the numerous and important errors of your Father's reign; directed the public wishes to the royal couch with a fervor little short of idolatry; and hailed the King's recovery as a national salvation?—No; it was the dread of seeing the government of the country degraded, by being committed to a cabal,—of which I shall give some description.

As it may be necessary to allude to A LADY, I
hope

hope nothing can escape me, that may be interpreted into injustice, or indelicacy to a sex, which is under too many disadvantages from the customs and laws of the land. Though I am old, I have not lost my memory of the rapturous season of love. I am incapable of an act so dastardly, as to sully the fame, or wound the peace of a woman.

It it not with love; it is with artifice and ambition, I am at war—and they are of no sex.

When you felt the fascinations of the *Perdita*, prudence smiled, and the error was justified by taste: but Cleopatra never saw, never will see in Anthony, any thing besides the probable master of the world.

Every measure, from the first moment of acquaintance, has been systematic: the experienced dame practised from art the lesson which Nature taught Daphne; she fled, that Apollo might follow: and by combining a slight and fickle inclination with Royal impatience, she formed a passion, which had been in vain attempted by charms and talents infinitely superior.

These things would not have been worth the trouble of recording, if the great object of the system had not been political power.

You

You will perceive the truth, if your Royal Highness will recollect, when impelled by filial duty to attend your Royal Parent on a sick bed, the Lady fixed herself at Bagshot, under the sympathetic wing of a Royal D——ss, and attended by her *faithful, disinterested friends,* Mr. and Mrs. Sheridan.

On this occasion the CABAL was formed, which with some variations in its members subsists to this time, and consists of—a *very great* Duchess, a fair and plump Lady of great ambition, Capt. P—, B— P——t, Mr. and Mrs. Sh——n, &c.

Conceive, Sir, the public sentiment, when a question of the utmost importance was depending, no access to your Royal Highness could be obtained no message delivered, nor a word spoken, without the knowledge of one or more of these *respectable* Personages. The nation lost all judgment on the subjects under consideration: the people saw only the cabal: the little White House in Pall-mall was regarded with the feelings of Syracuse at the ear of Dionysius; and the Minister might have marched his parliamentary adherents over propositions more absurd and pernicious, than those which assigned to prepared majorities, in a vicious and inadequate representation, prefentation, the whole political power of a free ftate.

The projected Court of the Regent did not efcape the public knowledge; and the *great* Duchefs had planned it on the model of that of Comus. The LADY was to be ennobled, to have her evening drawing rooms, in the manner of the Countefs of Yarmouth, and the modes of venality which diftinguifhed the politics of that favourite would not have been inexpedient to the circumftances, or unfuitable to the principles of the Cabal.

To accuftom the public eye to the purpofed inverfion of rank and order, the great Duchefs introduced the Lady into the acceffible purlieus of royalty, and fhe was frequently difplayed, as one of its poffible appendages, within the envied rails of Rotten-row. I faw the effect of that difplay on the crowd which obferved it: and if Pitt or Dundas had formed the ftratagem, it could not have been more to their purpofe. The heads of all the firft families in the kingdom were offended at the appearance of Sheridan in the fore ground, during the preparatory tranfactions for a Regency; but their WIVES and DAUGHTERS felt an infult when the great Duchefs conveyed the

Lady

Lady in triumph to breathe the royal dust of Rottenrow.

This is another instance of the judgment of your counsellors, who discern not that important consequences often arise from little causes.—No circumstance operated more rapidly and effectually than this incident on the zeal and attachment of the most respectable of your friends.

Since the Recovery of your Royal Father, these friends just save appearances: they frequently express apprehensions, that the habit of admitting and favoring witlings, buffoons, fidlers, fencers, and bruisers, will continue too long, and fix your character with the public. Henry V. to whom your Royal Highness is frequently compared, indulged his eccentricities at eighteen: your Royal Highness is approaching the age of thirty. Henry's Companions and his DOLL TEARSHEET were the revellers of an hour: your Royal Highness is invested by an interested, sordid set; their advice, their suggestions, their measures, would be a profanation of every thing princely: the modes of expence, the stratagems for obtaining money, the intermixture of *Royal spies*

*spies** and princely confidants, the familiarities of adventurers, &c. are not respectable, and being long continued, impress on the nation an idea of characteristic and incurable frivolity. This idea has been entertained by the most enlightened and valuable of your former friends; and their absence from your private parties, or nocturnal consultations, has given an artful and designing adventurer an opportunity of raising himself into consequence, to the great offence of those old and respectable families who actually placed on the throne the House of Brunswick, and supported it against foreign and domestic foes at a great expence of blood and treasure.

I entreat your Royal Highness to consider the circumstances which menace the peace and prosperity of this country, however advantageous its present situation.

It has escaped the precipice to which the American war had brought it, by a concurrence of events in Europe, to which it has not contributed by its talents or measures; though folly may ascribe them to

---

* Miss B— P—t and Capt. P—— are in the family without appointments, and hope to be the Madame Schwellenburgh and Jenkinson of Carlton House.

its

its Minifters and Councils: thofe events will foon have their effects; and a ftate of general peace, which even war muft fhortly produce, will favour that general difpofition in Europe for which philofophy has been long preparing it; which muft foon reach this ifland; and the nature of which I have undertaken to explain to you.

To contemplate this difpofition, to mark its approaches, and to judge of its effects, may be an employment as worthy your abilities, as it may be interefting to your future fate.

But this is not to be done among the puerile and petty diftractions of your prefent fituation. Confent to the wifhes of your Royal Parents—yield to the earneft defires of your country, by a marriage becoming your dignity, and by the eftablifhment of a refpectable houfehold: and then your Royal Highnefs may look forward, with thoughtful confideration, to the incidents and duties that probably await you.

LESSON III.

What! what! if they go on at this rate, in thirty years they will not leave a King in Europe.

GEORGE III.

IF his Majesty meant arbitrary kings, or persons invested with numerous discretionary powers, I am inclined to adopt the opinion.

Whether the executive power of the State should be in one or in many, is not with me a question: but that the executive should controul, direct, or influence the legislative; or that any species of power, prerogative, or privilege should be independent of the public will, is a question to which the abilities of the world seem at this time to be directed.

If your Royal Highness would but very cursorily examine the History of Europe, you would find, in almost every page, instances and acts of power, prerogative,

rogative, and privilege, to the disadvantage and injury of society. These acts have excited convulsions, which have been denominated rebellion or patriotism, according to their effects. It seems at this time to be the general purpose of political philosophy—not to expel or degrade constitutional kings—but to demolish those spurious and pernicious beings which are the offspring of privilege, and whose operations are capricious, arbitrary, and mischievous.

The great inquiry before the philosophical world is—not the nature of God, the mechanism of the universe, or the composition of its elements; but the principles of society. The world has been flooded with the blood of its inhabitants, by the caprices of tyrants, under the denomination of emperor, king, consul, senate, parliament, and popular assembly; and the miseries of millions demand of wisdom,
" Where is the power which establishes and con-
" nects all the orders of a community, and on which
" they all depend ? Where is the centre to which
" every thing tends, the principle from which all is
" derived, the sovereign that can do every thing ?
" Who can point out to us the form, the organi-
" zation

" zation of that moral perfon, a fociety or commu-
" nity, to which unity is neceffary, and of which
" Liberty is the effect?"

What anfwers have been made to this demand, may deferve the attention of your Royal Highnefs; as it may enable you to form an opinion on the King's prediction.

The fophiftry of political writers has been exhaufted on the comparative merits of monarchies, ariftocracies, and democracies; but no model has been exhibited, no form delineated, of a fociety which may protect and defend with its whole force the perfon and property of every one of its members, and in which each individual, by uniting himfelf to the whole, fhall neverthelefs be obedient only to himfelf, and remain fully at liberty to every thing but injury.

The general refult, however, of inquiry and experiment on political fubjects is,—an opinion or principle, that the fupreme power of every ftate is in the body of the people; becaufe it can have no intereft contrary to that of individuals, and ftands not in need of guarantees: for it is impoffible the body fhould attempt to hurt itfelf, or have a difpofition to injure its members.

But

But how is the general will to be obtained? Individuals may have private wills regarding private interest; but the general will is directed only to the general good.

History will not greatly assist us. Despotic and monarchic states are out of the inquiry. Indeed every lawful government is necessarily a REPUBLIC; for no other can have the public interest for its object: but those denominated republics in ancient and modern history, have not the public interest for their object, and are not formed to promote it. Athens, Lacedemon, and Rome were ruled by idle and profligate mobs in contention with privileged senates. Aristotle seems to prefer the constitution of Carthage to any other; but he justly observes, it was highly reprehensible, because the same person might be appointed to several offices; and a certain revenue or birth was necessary to civil situations—virtue being estimated as nothing.

Modern politics have admitted, in a few states, that the general voice should have a mode of expressing itself, and that the mode should be a part of the constitution: this has given rise to the idea of representation and the appointment of deputies.

But the supreme power or the actual sovereignty of a state cannot be represented or deputed. Powers may be delegated of various and extensive effect; but the omnipotence of society, if any where, is in itself. In the attempt to delegate sovereign power, the community would consign to its princes or its parliaments the disposition of life and property—on what condition? That they may dispose of them as they please.

The act which constitutes government is not, cannot be even a contract; it is the will, the arbitrary law, of an absolute sovereign. -The depositaries of delegated power, whether called princes, senates, or parliaments, are not proprietors or masters, they are subject to the people, who form and support the society; by an eternal law of nature, which has ever subjected a part to the whole.

But your Royal Highness may say, Why perplex me with such inquiries? " I have always been " instructed, the constitution of England is the " utmost effort of human wisdom; and I should " answer you by a reference to that constitution."

LESSON IV.

CONSTITUTION OF ENGLAND.

Cunctas nationes et urbes, populus aut primores aut finguli regunt. Delecta ex his et conftituta Reipub. forma, laudari facilius quam evenire; vel fi evenerit, haud diuturna effe poteft. *Tac.*

All nations and cities are governed either by the people, the nobles, or by fingle rulers. A Republic conftituted by an union of thefe, is to be wifhed for rather than accomplifhed, or if accomplifhed, it would not be lafting.

THIS is fuppofed to be the plan, on which the conftitution of England is formed; but the fuppofition is groundlefs. The Englifh government has fluctuated more than any other in Europe; and the fluctuations have been wholly owing to the operation of moral and political Incidents.

Violent imprudences of defpotifm produced fome apparent and fome real improvements in the adminiftration of law; but the conftitution of the legiflature

lature is a fraudulent deception; and the people of England have in reality no more choice or will in the election of their pretended reprefentatives, than the people of Hinduftan, Perfia, or Turkey.

Let your Royal Highnefs be at the trouble of looking into Middlefex and Weftminfter; and no parts of England are fo free—deduct from the electors all the tradefmen who are obliged to vote with their cuftomers; the tenants who are appendages to houfes; and the freeholders who are entangled with the ariftocracy or with government: and you may be furprized at the remainder.

Sir—a free people, that can neither form itfelf into a community, nor execute any operation; but is abfolutely fubjected in its actions and energies, and in the fubjects on which it is permitted to think and fpeak—to powers conftitutionally fubordinate—is an abfurdity.

No people can be free, whofe deputies may be enflaved by the executive power, who fee the pretended conftitution and laws refigned to its mercy; without being able to oppofe any things but petitions and complaints to thofe who have an intereft in the abufes.

If

If I wished to give a summary of the English constitution, as it has existed some time in practice, I would not make extracts from the romances of Montesquieu or Blackstone—I would invoke the PIOUS muse of a Marquis Townshend or of an Edmund Burke, when warmed by the long-sought rays of royal favour: and as every thing is at this time covered by religion, I would place the most popular of your ancestors—and each in his day has been called THE BEST OF KINGS—before the GOD * OF ISRAEL, to whom he should offer the following devotions:

"If it hath been OUR object to dispute with an
"aristocracy the government of a people who support us, and to render liberty, property, and life
"at the discretion of disciplined majorities, in those
"assemblies which should protect them—if to secure
"a sure though imperceptible dominion over the legislature, and to add the power of making to that
"of executing the laws—secrecy and craft have been
"substituted for authority and power: thou wilt for-

---

* To what are we to ascribe, that priests never address *national* prayers to the God of Nature, Truth, and Virtue?

"give

" give the neceffity, as in the moft favoured of thy
" anointed fervants of ancient times.

" We thank thee, that the affiduity and labour
" of many years have not been fruitlefs; and that
" we have A LOYAL AND DUTIFUL PARLIAMENT.
" To fuit temptations to the vain, the ambitious,
" the needy; to practife the various arts which in-
" fluence vicious affemblies; to have the fuppofed
" reprefentatives of the people *in the confidence* of
" our fervants; to induce them to declaim on na-
" tional interefts, while they propofe the indulgence
" of their paffions, to forget their country in defi-
" ance of engagements, yet to fave appearances, or
" even to affume the fame of virtue—Thefe are ob-
" jects of magnitude and merit. The penfioners of
" OUR court and their numerous connections; thofe
" who watch for occafional douceurs; thofe who
" make fpeeches to force ftipulations; and the fly-
" ing fquadrons which fluctuate between duty and
" temptation.—We thank thee, that we have no-
" thing to fear from fuch guardians.

" The grand fecret in the management of politi-
" cal bodies, is that of dividing them, and paffing the
" proftituted parts for the whole. Every thing is
" accom-

"accomplished, when the legislature is involved in
"the faction of the court, partaking OUR bounty, or
"hoping to partake it, and joining, in any measures,
"the puppet WE fix at the helm.——Foster, in thy
"goodness, the general disposition to servility: the
"SACRED tribe has ever been ready to diffuse pom-
"pous titles, sublime names, and divine honours, as
"involved in the ideas of royalty; and if the Prince
"consent to be their apparitor, to patronize their
"oppressions, or to execute their cruelties, they soon
"instruct the credulous multitude to consider him,
"as he may be, the representative of THEIR God,
"his decrees as oracles from heaven, and blind sub-
"mission as the most sacred duty. When Samuel
"hewed Agag into pieces, and when Nero mur-
"dered his mother, the priests led the people to the
"temples, to thank THEIR GODS for actions, and
"to offer incense for crimes, which human nature
"abhorred.

"The enchantment of superstition renders ser-
"viceable the most unprincipled and most infamous
"of men. On a national festival, the mouth of the
"congregation shall be the most celebrated for de-
"ception; the name being equivalent to a falsehood
"in

" in every spot of the world : yet the holy bandage
" is tinctured and transparent; it renders good evil,
" and evil good. The yoke of the priesthood,
" though the most galling, is the least hazardous of
" all the instruments of despotic power: that system
" of civil tyranny is the most practicable, which is
" grafted on affections supposed to be religious; and
" this, through the world, is the desired ALLIANCE
" OF CHURCH AND STATE.

" HISTORY furnishes lessons on the events attri-
" buted to thy providence. Our *pious* predecessor,
" Henry VII. now with thee, always ruled by a fac-
" tion; and, according to the *inspired* Burke, it is
" the constitutional government of the land. It is
" true, he erred in the open appointment of the Emp-
" son and Dudley of the day; for he did not mask
" their vices by ostensible innocence and honesty;
" the judicious interposition of unsullied purity and
" blunt brutality would have enabled them, as it
" enables the instruments of OUR power to pervert
" forms, and to distribute among OUR and THEIR
" friends the fruits of general industry.

" Cast a HOLY mist before the eyes of the peo-
" ple; give our ministers wisdom, to lull them into
" se-

" security. Let determined profligacy and profane-
" ness, in the most favoured of our servants, ap-
" pear as stern integrity; let juvenile ignorance be
" called candour, and the want of natural passions
" be deemed purity; and let a cautious system of
" avaricious artifice, which eradicates every fibre by
" which a child is held to a mother's heart, be cele-
" brated by all the bands of venality, as supernatu-
" ral and divine prudence.—The people never fore-
" see their fate: it is the peculiar faculty of our
" present servants to render illusive the birthright of
" Britons, and to undermine, by plausible pretences
" the most sacred liberties: the laborious peasant,
" or the industrious mechanic, perceives not his ser-
" vitude until he is sprinkled by the blood of his
" fellow-subject, or feels himself unexpectedly
" crushed.

" By the present system of finance, the interests
" of the treasury are so entwined with the general
" property, that it requires the most delicate hand
" to lay the axe at any of the roots of corruption.
" The most oppressive minister, if he use the lan-
" guage of reluctance and candour, may be effectu-
" ally supported by the numerous FACTORS of his
" admi-

"administration; by speculators in funds, by con-
"tractors, brokers, ticket dealers; by the timid,
"the weak, the fickle, the sordid, the indolent pos-
"sessors of money: these form powerful and ex-
"tensive factions in favor of the slightest whisper
"from the treasury; they raise clamours against the
"complaints of patriotism; and they smother the
"melancholy murmurs of the nation. Yet occa-
"sional difficulties arise. The wants of venality
"are infinite; and though we contract debts with
"one hand to accumulate with the other, the ava-
"rice of . . . . . . is an unfathomable and insatia-
"ble abyss.—Enlighten the soul of our HEAVEN-
"BORN minister with the strongest rays of inven-
"tion, but surround his heart with ice: let it never
"palpitate with any passion that does not spring
"from systematic depredation; let him be dead to
"all pleasure and all joy: he might otherwise be
"moved by pity at the cries of want in the fangs
"of excise. Concentrate all his affections in the
"ambition of serving us with the hope of immea-
"surable reward; confirm him in the exquisite hy-
"pocrisy by which fallacious hopes are held out,
"that the public burdens will be removed, and the
"pub-

"public vexations mitigated: may he live without
" ties, avoid the inconveniences of generous paf-
" fions, AND WE WILL EXTINGUISH HIS FAME,
" LIKE THE IMPOSTURE OF CHATHAM, BY RE-
" WARDS THAT SHALL RENDER HIM INFAMOUS!

" We thank thee, that by his affiduity, the arms
" of the cuftoms and excife nearly embrace the
" land. Inftruct their numerous retainers to infi-
" nuate the maxims of fubjection, to abufe by fear,
" to feduce by hope, to corrupt by avarice; to dif-
" fipate all averfion of power, and all horror of
" tyranny: to expatiate on OUR SACRED UNDER-
" TAKINGS; and to beftow encomiums on deeds
" which *profane*, and audacious patriotifm would
" brand with infamy.

" WE now hear little of fenfible, fober, or wife
" men; of that elevation which fcorns fervility to
" power; or of that generofity which, in every
" form, would efpoufe the caufe of Liberty: we
" fee only ambition, varioufly mafked, anxioufly
" marking the fources of wealth; wretches who
" hope to profper by public diforder; ATHEIS-
" TIC PRIESTS in the garb of piety, fervile aca-
" demicians, difputatious pedants, and the varie-
" gated

" gated herds of political and ecclesiastical prosti-
" tutes.

" Protect those societies, academies, schools, and
" universities, where every thing may be taught,
" except the DUTIES of kings, the rights of socie-
" ties, and the general privileges of mankind.

" Let the retainers of wisdom seek consolation
" in virtuous poverty; give us supple pensioners,
" brilliant sophists, and prostituted sycophants:
" the praises they bestow are profuse, and they fly
" on LAUREATED wings through every climate to
" cull the flowers of adulation; while obstinate in-
" tegrity suffers in silence, or the sighs of suffering
" virtue are enclosed by the walls of its wretched
" habitation.

" By the wisdom inspired by the GOD OF JACOB
" we have converted our bitterest enemy into a
" friend. The liberty of the press, our aversion
" and horror, is now our advantage; for instead of
" using the chicane and fraud of law, which are
" pernicious to friend and foe, we directed into that
" province OUR BENIGN AND ROYAL INFLUENCE:
" it instantly attracted the secondary swarms of li-
" terati, whose existence, like that of reptiles, de-

" pends

"pends on depredation and injury: deſtitute of vir-
"tue, they will not aſcribe it without reward; and
"their ſhafts of ridicule are poiſoned by envy; glo-
"rious deeds they depreſs with alacrity; good ac-
"tions ſicken them; and the friends of liberty they
"cordially aſperſe.——We laud and praiſe thee for
"mercenary ſcribblers in all the provinces of lite-
"rature. THOU HAST MADE NO VERMIN IN VAIN;
"thoſe who feed on our reputation and happineſs,
"as well as thoſe who burrow in our fleſh: their ef-
"forts are leſs offenſive than the villainies of law-
"yers in aſperſing popular and aſpiring men, when
"in oppoſition to the treaſury, and vilifying or de-
"faming thoſe who counteract the machinations of
"the cabinet.

"We thank thee for thoſe proſtituted multitudes
"ſo eaſily obtained in this town, who ſpread ru-
"mours, excite ſuſpicions, and ruin all public con-
"fidence in the pretenſions of virtue: thou haſt
"enabled us to deviſe thoſe ſnares which entangle
"popular characters, and induce them to diſgrace
"themſelves.

"Our PIOUS brother Louis XIV. when he wiſhed
"to deceive the French nation, had recourſe to
"feſ-

"festivals called religious, and the display of the fine arts, which encourage those only who subsist by the follies of the opulent, and the industry of whose professors attaches them to no country. While the inconsiderate multitude is devoted to joy, they perceive not the chains which WE cover with flowers; or the remote consequences that threaten them, and by which every controlling check on our power is to be cut down.

"By festivals, shews, and exhibitions, WISE politicians extinguished in Rome that restless love of liberty, so inconvenient to power. The progress of the arts has been ever accompanied with the progress of slavery, and even sciences of a sedentary and puerile kind have similar tendencies. Hence the servile devotion of academies, societies, and learned corporations.

"It requires the highest portion of wisdom from THEE to render the army tolerable to *seditious* Englishmen; soldiers have been GRADUALLY substituted every where for civil officers; they arrest offenders, they attend malefactors, or they clear the highways; they are placed at the entrance of theatres, auction and exhibition rooms; "they

" they watch the people wherever they meet, and
" serve as nightly guards where any thing valuable
" is to be guarded: they have tried insults and in-
" juries on the people, who are not suffered to de-
" fend themselves.—When the whole of this good
" work is perfected, OUR soul will sing hallelujah
" to THEE, O GOD OF ARMIES!

" In this complicated system of policy, if any
" errors are committed, thou knowest WE CAN
" DO NO WRONG; the blame is on bad councellors.
" Let the evils of a detestable and disgraceful war
" be on Lord ———; WE have changed OUR ad-
" ministration; and if WE succeed not in any of
" OUR views by the instrumentality of OUR pre-
" sent servants, WE will repent of the unsuccess-
" ful measures, dismiss the unsuccessful minister
" with the guilt of failure on his head; and, with-
" out the apprehension of future consequences,
" direct all OUR high priests to call the GOD OF
" ISRAEL to witness OUR intentions. In all these
" things WE trace the steps of the PIOUS MARTYR,
" and of ALL THE NURSING FATHERS AND NUR-
" SING MOTHERS OF THY CHURCH."

But I will delineate the English Constitution more explicitly, than can be done by any imitation of the present fashionable devotion.

LESSON

LESSON V.

THE SUBJECT CONTINUED.

When Princes, who ought to be common parents, make themselves a party, and lean to a side—it is a boat that is overthrown by uneven weight.   Lord Bacon.

WITH all the boasted learning and improvement of mankind, no society has been yet so constituted or organized as to produce that genuine public principle, whose object is the security and happiness of the community.

As men emerge from savage into civilized conditions, some species of talents obtain a preference, and the general labour is taxed to support privileges, or to fulfil the iniquitous and monstrous engagements of hereditary and perpetual rewards.

Hence the origin of dignities, ranks, and families; the various combinations of which have formed all the governments of Europe.

The gradations of moderate oppression, or of cruel tyranny in those governments, have been owing to the various modes of combination or conspiracy in the oppressors; and those modes have been inaccurately, but commonly denominated CONSTITUTIONS.

I wish not to teize your Royal Highness on the supposed origin and structure of the English government: it has no other origin than that of all artifices, to subject the general industry to the caprice, convenience, and pleasure of fortunate adventurers. The internal agitations of states and their external wars, though attributed to other causes, have been wholly owing to the operations of these combinations, or to competitions for their unjustifiable prerogatives.

When the Saxons had subdued England, they instituted as many governments as there were powerful heads of armies; the common soldiers of which they admitted to privileges, on the condition of holding in the most wretched slavery the peasants of the country: this extended the privileged combinations widely; and the jarring interests, claims, and principles produced by the union of the heptarchy, furnished

nished the vigorous and comprehensive mind of Alfred with the first correct and rational idea of a political constitution which is recorded in history.

The circumstances of the country requiring the steady and continued exertion of its utmost force, he had the genius to discern,—the exertion of that force could not be obtained but by the actual concurrence and exercise of the general will: he, therefore, organized the free parts of the community into a political constitution, the best imagined and the most effectual that has hitherto been exhibited in the world.

To save your Royal Highness the trouble of discovering this invention by my description, I will exhibit it in a diagram.

By an attentive glance your Royal Highnefs may underftand the excellences and defects of this wonderful fabric, and learn to revere the memory of a prince, who, in an age deemed dark and ignorant, could look farther into a fcience which has hitherto baffled the ftrongeft efforts of human reafon, than any philofopher or ftatefman of ancient or modern times.

Your Royal Highnefs will obferve, there can be but two fpecies of government—by the general will, or by the will of one or more perfons controuling the general will. The latter, in all poffible variations, not being juftified by reafon, the neceffary principles of juftice, or by experience—a general acknowledgment has been obtained, that the reafonable, equitable, and beneficial principle of every political conftitution is the public will: but the mode of forming or obtaining that will, was a problem inexplicable until it attracted the powers of the immortal Alfred.

The political ftructure of that great prince has all the neceffary properties and effects of an organized body. The head and the extremities are united; not by occafional elections, or by pretended
dele-

Plate 1.

POLITICAL CONSTITUTION of ENGLAND by ALFRED.

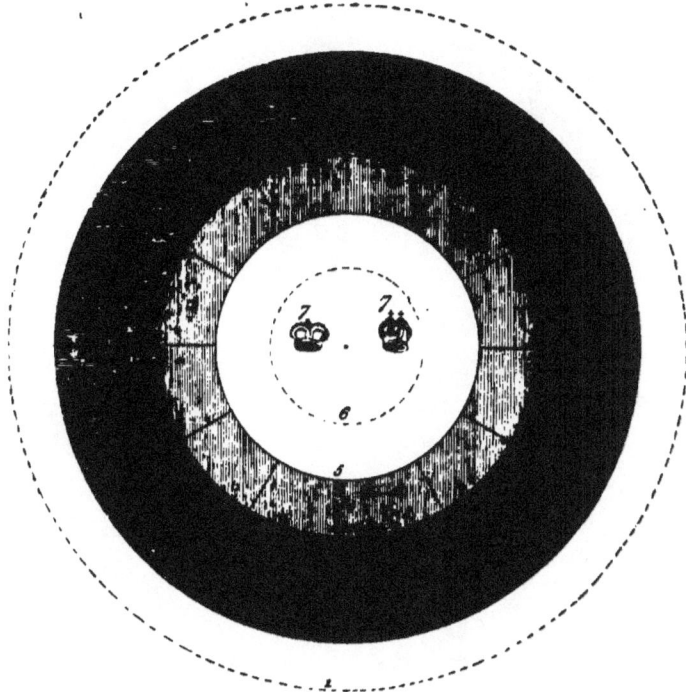

1. Peasants in Slavery.
2. Freemen in Tythings actually electing their Tything Men annually
3. Judges, Magistrates & Commanders of the Hundreds elected by the Tything Men annually.
4. Commanders & Magistrates of Counties elected annually by those of the Hundreds.
5. The Mycle-Gemot, Folk-mote, or annual Assembly of all the Freemen in the Nation, in which the ordinary Acts of the Legislature & Government were adjudged.
6. Wittenagemot – The ordinary Legislature consisting of the King, Barons, Bishops &c.
7. The Executive & Ecclesiastical Powers co-ordinate.

delegations of national power. The whole surface of the body, by minute subdivision, is formed to receive and transmit instantaneous impressions, external and internal; all the parts are held to their offices by the general force, without commotion and without violence; and the public will being enforced by the public strength, is a law which nothing in the community can dispute or resist.

Two diseases remained in the actual society organized by Alfred, which his power could not eradicate, but which the political constitution would have gradually expelled—the superstitious dominion of ecclesiastics, and the slavery of the peasants. The appointment of ecclesiastics, by any species of patronage, is absolutely inconsistent with public liberty, as it is with the private honour and virtue of those who are appointed; and the community that admits of slavery, even in the most obscure and unfortunate of its members, is a monster, the offspring of ignorance or injustice.

The successors of Alfred inherited not his genius; and the general confusion and misery which ensued on his decease, impaired the structure he had formed: the Norman conquest completed its ruin, and a mode of of government took place, in which the general will was not confulted.

The internal agitations of the ftate, from the Conqueft to the Revolution, were thofe of princes and barons, as competitors for a prize, or as beafts for prey: and if your Royal Highnefs will candidly confider the celebrated Revolution, you will find it a compact between the Prince and Princefs of Orange, and the heads of certain families, attended by the Mayor of London and other perfons in the exercife of authority.

I have no doubt, that the meafure had the general approbation; but the nation had no ORGAN by which it might form or exprefs the public will: defpotifm and violence had decompofed it as a body; and factions, more or lefs exceptionable, affumed its name, offices, and privileges.

Government for fome time was conducted by the advice, direction, or influence of the great families, which placed the houfes of Orange and Brunfwic on the throne; long poffeffion formed the idea of an hereditary claim in thofe families to occupy the principal offices of the ftate; and a refiftance to that claim, by perfons who had no farther views than

than to participate its advantages, has occafioned all the factions and contentions of the late reigns.

The government of England—FOR ENGLAND HAS NO POLITICAL CONSTITUTION—may be thus delineated:

Englifh

By comparing this diagram with the ſtructure of Alfred, your Royal Highneſs muſt perceive the difference between a whole nation organized into a political body or conſtitution, and any internal machinery at the will of one or more perſons, to affect, to influence, or enſlave the ſociety: the firſt is, Prometheus a moral agent at liberty, and conferring bleſſings on the world; the other is, the vulture feeding on his liver, while his body is chained to a rock.

If this diſtinction were univerſally underſtood, political and civil Liberty would be univerſally eſtabliſhed. If the whole ſociety be not ſo arranged, conſtructed, or organized, as to produce general animation, life, will, force, judgment, and reaſon, analogous to thoſe of the natural body, there can be no liberty.

This is the reaſon, that ancient and modern inſtitutions, very improperly called republics, are as unproductive of general happineſs as governments denominated deſpotic: and not any obſtacles to the aptitude or native talents of one order more than another for precedence and dominion. Diſcretionary power is tyranny, whether in a populace, in a ſenate,

ENGLISH GOVERNMENT at the REVOLUTION.

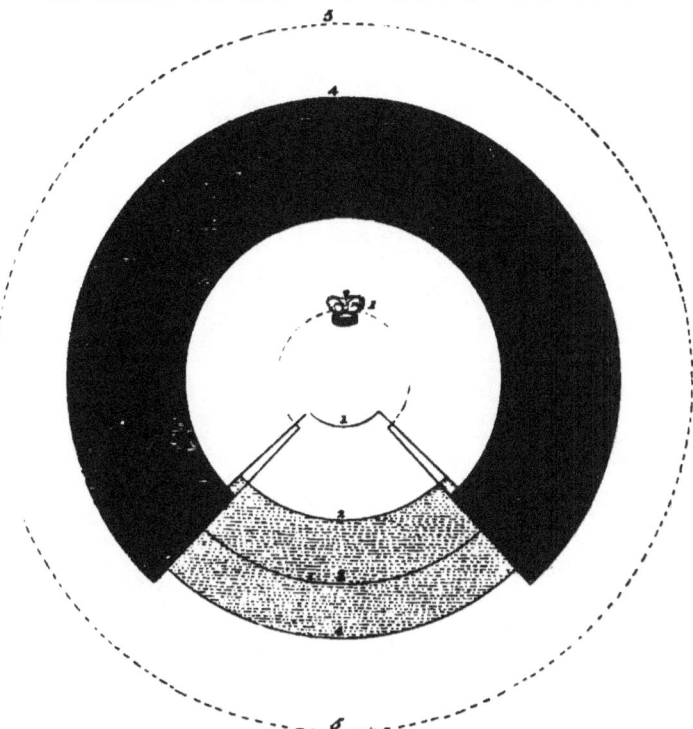

1. The Aristocracy unequally divided; the Majority having the Crown in tutelage.
2. The Legislature unequally divided & appointed by the unequal divisions of the Aristocracy.
3. Lord Lieutenants, Sheriffs, Archbishops, Bishops &c. appointed by the Aristocracy: the Majority using the Name of the Crown.
4. Justices of the Peace, Rectors, Vicars &c. appointed by the Aristocracy, Lord-Lieutenants &c.
5. The body of the People variously operated upon, & amused by forms; but having really no election or choice and no share in the Political Government.

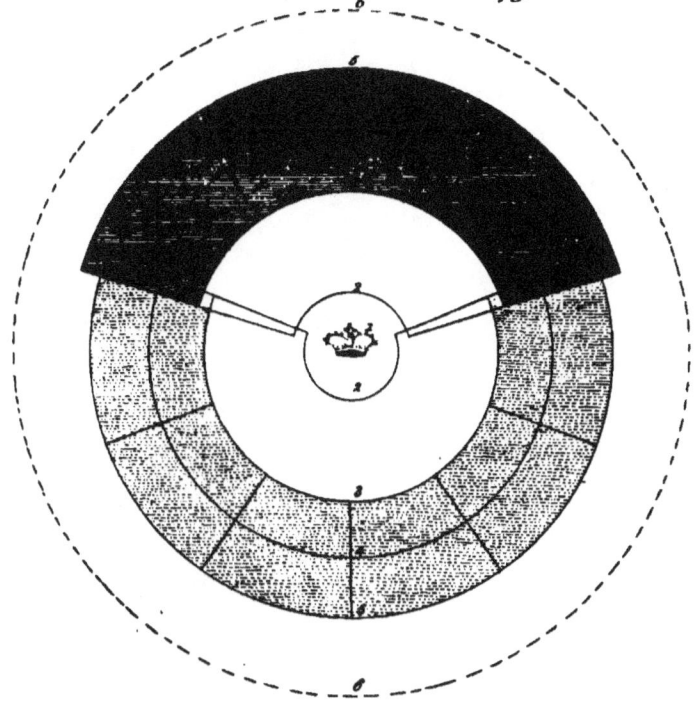

1. The Crown considerably emancipated & influencing a small majority of the Aristocracy.
2. The Aristocracy divided almost equally.
3. The Legislature appointed by the Crown & the Aristocracy; & influenced & divided in the same manner.
4. Lord Lieutenants, Archbishops, Bishops, &c. appointed influenced & divided in the manner of Parliament.
5. Justices of the Peace, Rectors, Vicars &c. appointed, influenced & divided by their Patrons.
6. The Body of the People, variously operated upon, & amused by forms, but having no election, choice, or share in the Political Government.

nate, in a nobility, or in a King; as the force and will of the body would be inconvenient and deftructive, if wholly confined to the feet, the hands, or the head.

Alfred, alone among political inventors, feems to have fully comprehended the nature and properties of fociety, as a moral body or EFFECTIVE CONSTITUTION.

In his ftructure, the houfeholders are fubdivided on the furface, and form the external fenfes, the origin of all ideas. The mycle-gemot is the feat of the mind; where the ideas are combined into thoughts; and where the will, the judgment, and reafon, direct the active or executive powers. Here no competitions can arife among ranks and orders; becaufe all the parts, however externally diftinguifhed, are, like the members of the natural body, directed and impelled by the general animating principle, the general will, and the general intereft.

The Englifh nation at this time is not arranged, conftructed, or organized into a political body. All its houfholders have not even nominal votes. They who are faid to poffefs the privilege, are controlled or directed in the exercife of it, by various orders
affect-

affecting to be their superiors. The ideas of this pretended body therefore do not originate in the external senses.

A factitious body is generated within the society, which assumes the denomination of the state: but not being in sympathy with all the parts, often acts in direct opposition to the general feeling, inclination, or interest, which is the actuating principle or fundamental law of every free community.

LESSON

LESSON VI.

SPECULATIONS.

" I have been taught, not to submit implicitly to have in view actions
"which are deemed practicable, but those which may have more
"of the possibility of wishes than the probability of execution;
"and to undertake them when the circumstances of time and
"power seem most favorable."

THE struggles of factions in England were always conducted under plausible pretences. The Tories professed exalted opinions of the prerogatives of Kings and the privileges of Ecclesiastics; and were the votaries of despotism slightly disguised. The Whigs wore a better masque: for they readily allowed the people the forms of election and the appearance of representation, but rendered those forms and appearances ineffectual or mischievous to the community by the modes of conducting or influencing them—They protected the church, as the best instrument of corrupt measures; and by this circumstance alone they

they checked that progress of political knowledge and that love of liberty, which would probably have restored the constitution of Alfred.

I will explain myself, lest your Royal Highness should imagine me a sectary: a denomination I abhor.

Partial toleration of opinions, like the partial liberty of the press, produced mischief instead of advantage. Numerous sects appeared in rancorous competition with each other, and in implacable hostility to their common oppressor, the Church.

When any effort was made to obtain redress of grievances, civil or religious, the sectaries crowded the standard of reformation: some artful priest founded the trumpet of bigotry, impressed an idea of danger to the Church; and the best intentions for public advantage were involved in the general odium of sectaries.

These artifices were penetrated by philosophers—the great benefactors of the world. Mr. Locke wrote a treatise on Government; Montesquieu the Spirit of Laws; Hume scattered hints in Essays; Rousseau blended profound truths and brilliant sophisms in the Social Compact; Steuart collected the

impor-

important science of Europe into the Inquiry on Political Oeconomy; and Adam Smith pointed out the channels by which industry conveyed or accumulated wealth.

Great as the talents of these philosophers may be deemed, and considerable as the services they have rendered the world: they have not at all considered, or they have left in doubt and uncertainty, the problem most important to the happiness of mankind, and which an ancient sage* has thus expressed, " The only skill and knowledge of any value in " politics is that of governing All by All."

The government of England exhibited to their view every actual effect of despotism, while it preserved the forms and even the reputation of Liberty. They proposed temporary remedies for partial evils; but no man furnished a plain, practicable idea of a free Constitution, a society organized into a moral body, animated by principles, and directed by its own will.—Mr. Locke's observations are in favour of liberty: but they are general. They state rights which oppressive governments may not dispute: but

---

* Heraclitus.

the mode of asserting, recovering, or preserving them, he does not point out. His mind had not conceived the general and certain remedy of social disorders and the only origin of Political Liberty, in the formation of the whole society into a moral being.

Montesquieu, as a philosophical historian, is extremely valuable: as a politician, he is useless or he is pernicious. The opinion that climate should produce and modify government, is fanciful, perhaps puerile; but the idea that any natural and necessary cause should generate A SLAVE, is unphilosophic, untrue, and detestable.

Mr. Hume had talents for political inquiries; but he was principally solicitous for his own fortune and his own fame: his temper and heart were cold; and he apologized for tyranny with as much zeal, as he would have felt in describing the destruction of the Bastile, or the demolition of the infernal dungeons of the Inquisition.

In the enumeration of the origin and effects of moral causes, Hume is a philosopher; in the following important opinion, I fear he is an interested sophist: " It will be found, if I mistake not, that " the

" the two extremes in government, Liberty and Sla-
" very, commonly approach neareſt to each other;
" and that as you depart from the extremes, and
" mix a little *Monarchy* with Liberty, the govern-
" ment always becomes *free* and *è contra*," Eſſay II.
—In the fourth Eſſay he calls it an " *univerſal* ax-
" iom, that an hereditary prince, a nobility without
" vaſſals, and a people voting by their repreſenta-
" tives, form the beſt monarchy, ariſtocracy, and
" democracy."

In his idea of a perfect commonwealth, there are many uſeful ameliorations of what is called the Engliſh Conſtitution; and in the laſt quotation I ſhall ſubmit from his works, he ſhuns the great difficulty of the queſtion under conſideration, for a reaſon which may make your Royal Highneſs ſmile —" Having intended in this Eſſay, (XV.) to make
" a full compariſon of civil liberty and abſolute go-
" vernment, and to have ſhewn the great advan-
" tages of the former above the latter, I began to
" ſuſpect, *that no man in this age* was ſufficiently qua-
" lified for this undertaking; and that whatever any
" one ſhould advance, would in all probability be
" re-

" refuted by farther experience, and be rejected by
" posterity."

Rousseau's heart atoned for the caprices of his head; and his sensibility to injury, if committed on a worm, drew his penetrating eye into the recesses of political intrigue.

Though the supposition of social compact, the foundation of his treatise, be wholly fanciful, for the idea of a political constitution is produced like that of a wheelbarrow,* it is wonderful how frequently he approaches the truth.

" When the people have chosen deputies, are
" they defunct, are they annihilated? Though they
" cannot speak by the laws, they *should* have a
" mode of attending to their administration."—
" The general voice should have a mode of exert-
" ing itself, or it is useless, and that mode should
" be *part of the Constitution:* the whole of the State
" should ever accompany the general Will."

---

* I do not mean any thing ludicrous or degrading by this allusion: but that, as men discovered the use of the wheelbarrow by reason and experience, they discover the principles of Government in the same manner: and principles are applied to a society to form a Constitution, as those of mechanics are applied to iron, or timber, to form machines.

This

This idea was suggested to Rousseau by the periodical councils of Geneva, which had a power to oblige the magistrates and all the orders of the State to confine themselves within the bounds prescribed by arrangements denominated the Constitution.

He observes, " The general Will should flow " from All to be applicable to All—every one sub" jects himself to the conditions he imposes on " others: this is equitable, because common to all; " useful, because it can have no object but the ge" neral good; and durable, because resting on the " public strength."—But,

" Hath the body politic an organ to make known " its Will?—The general will is always in the " right; but the judgment by which it is directed, " is not always sufficiently informed.—Individuals " often see the good they reject; the public is de" sirous of that which it may be incapable of re" ceiving: both equally stand in need of a guide. " Hence arises the necessity of a legislator." B. II. c. 6.

Rousseau is thus beautifully and pertinently sententious; but his genius leaves him, where alone its exertions could have essentially benefitted society:

he is taken up by his declamatory dæmon; refers to Plato and Lycurgus; and wishes for deities to regulate affairs which are allotted only to mortals. The principles and maxims he has scattered through his treatise, are all invalidated by a declaration, that " to investigate those conditions of society which " may best answer the purposes of nations, would " require the abilities of some superior intelligence, " who should be witness to all the passions of men, " but be subject to none. He who undertakes to " form a body politic, ought to perceive himself " capable of working a total change in human na-" ture."—He does not bear in mind, that government is the principal instrument of that change; and that the public will, being expressed by a permanent Constitution, would form that public judgment and public reason, by the necessity of reflection on the events it produced: effects would become causes, and errors instructions.

The Inquiry of Sir James Steuart is learned and profound; but it is clogged with prejudices, and obscured by a stile uncouth and almost unintelligible; it has therefore been of more utility to authors than to the public:—and Adam Smith, with inferior

powers

powers and less information, but with more art of arrangement, and greater perspicuity of language, has attracted more attention, and been of greater service in stimulating political inquiries—But no plan similar to that of Alfred had been suggested to controul the despotism of all discretionary delegations, and to conduct the community by the impulse of its own will, when the American Revolution invited political philosophers to display their talents and knowledge.

As I would distinguish speculations from facts, I shall render the Constitutions of the American States the materials of another Lesson.

LESSON

LESSON VII.

THE AMERICAN REVOLUTION.

Numa religionibus et divino jure populum devinxit.
Tac. Ann. iii. 36.

Truths are never controverted with passion and malignity, if not enjoined as articles of belief. In the demonstrative sciences, truths not universally understood are not received, and never enjoined, though immediately tending to public advantage. It would be thus in religious inquiries, if religion were left by men as it is left by God.—Your Royal Highness will easily imagine, I do not mean by the word God any of those immoral, mischievous, malignant phantoms the patrons of particular nations, whether Jews or Gentiles—I do not mean any of the divinities, with whom the most exceptionable of your ancestors have affected particular intimacies

—I do

—I do not mean any of the beings who may be called upon by venal and unprincipled priests, to throw the varied veils of contradictory superstitions over the infernal intrigues which may tinge the earth with human blood from the shores of the Danube to Nootka Sound—I mean the God of *all* nature, of *all* mankind—of whose existence no mind can doubt, without being involved in inextricable absurdities—but

> " In search of whom, o'erstretched idea bursts,
> " And thought rolls back on darkness."——

The power, wisdom, and goodness of this ineffable Power have been associated with the most pernicious vices, in the characters of an indefinite number of gods; the fear and worship of which have been deemed necessary auxiliaries to various forms of political government. The superstition being involved in the constitution, sometimes its instrument, sometimes its *director*, it was sheltered from the approaches of reason or inquiry by the supposed expedience of supporting that Constitution.—Among the successful impostures of this kind, the Roman Catholic superstition

perstition is remarkable: it approached the civil government in the garb of lowly meekness and disinterested humility; it sought toleration, then protection, then dominion; it nearly obtained the wish of Caligula; for mankind seemed to have one neck, on which it set its foot.

In any institution, as in any private mind, the spirit of intolerance and persecution is in proportion to its opposition to reason and the enormity of its absurdities. The cruelties of the church of Rome have, therefore, been so horrible, that they will leave on the character of human nature a stain which no time or virtue can efface.

When the oppressions of this pernicious despotism became intolerable, some ameliorations took place, under pretences of reformation, on the general principle, *that in order to preserve the profits and advantages of ecclesiastical imposture, some of its most enormous and shameful abuses should be relinquished.*

Hence the moderation and prudence of ecclesiastical policies denominated reformed; and those qualities are to be found among sectaries in a graduated state, as their power is diminished, or they are forced

forced by reciprocal contentions towards the confines of reason. But in all Christian sects, the Quakers only excepted, the principle of persecution is to be discerned, under some pretence or disguise, and in a dormant or active state; and it will ever remain, while a single privileged impostor, whether he be called a Pope, a Bishop, a Dissenting Clergyman, or a Methodist Exhorter, can find advantage in annexing or affecting to annex merit or demerit to the belief of any propositions.

In the institution of the Church of England, the English reformers could not agree on *all* the Popish abuses to be relinquished, and the Puritan faction arose, which has continued to this time, under various forms, the faithful repository of interested discontent, virulent zeal for favourite opinions, and a sincere, though generally mistaken love of Liberty.

In the clumsy engine called the English Government at the Reformation, the Church had considerable effect, and was an important part. Government, therefore, exercised severities on those who disturbed its operations, and the foundations of the American states were laid by a species of intolerance

in

in England, the natural produce of an ill-constructed and vicious constitution.

It would lead me too far out of my way to trace the character of each American state in its origin; in the objects, manners, and institutions of its first planters; and in the succeeding operations of their various charters.

This is an inquiry as important to an American statesman, as it would be instructive to the world—But I only wish to point out to your Royal Highness, that an American, drawing in with his first breath a just abhorrence of those aristocratic and ecclesiastic privileges, which held Europe in perpetual warfare, oppression, and misery—and the American states having happily defeated all the arts of Britain to introduce them under any pretences, or in any forms—it may be expected, their constitutions would be considerable improvements on that of England. By a candid and fair examination, this expectation will not be greatly disappointed.

On the emancipation of America, she exhibited several extraordinary characters; and the multitude is ever disposed to ascribe great events to reputed

great

great men: than which there is not an error more pernicious in the regions of credulity.

The Americans became free by exercifing a very moderate portion of paffive prudence, and that prudence was the offspring of neceffity. Wafhington acted the part of Fabius, becaufe he had not Fabius's army; for the Americans would often have fought; and by fighting have loft their country.

With Franklin I was in great intimacy, when that event was ftruggling in the womb.—I fpeak not from fancy, but from certain knowledge, that he fincerely wifhed to prevent it; and when forced into political negociations, for which he had no talents, his merit confifted in prudent patience. The Revolution of America was completely managed in England; and its principal authors were Lord Bute, Lord North Lord Sackville, and Mr. Jenkinfon. The American war originated in parliamentary jobbing; and its great purpofe was to transfer enormous maffes of Englifh property into loans, funds, and taxes, to form that corrupt minifterial phalanx called the Friends of Government. While this faction, like a malignant difeafe, was draining the vital fubftances of Britain, and even armies and
navies

navies were merely its ramifications; the cabinet of France obeyed the fentiments of the nation without intending to gratify it, and America obtained its liberty.

When the leaders of the American States affembled to form the Conftitution of the Republic, not òne of them difcovered the genius of a great ftatefman. But the American character ferved them on that occafion: they had patience; information flowed in from every part of the world; and they formed with confiderable fkill the federative conftitution of the American States.

In this great event, it is but juftice to obferve, that the perfons moft celebrated were not the moft ufeful; that almoft all important hints were taken from communications, the authors of which may never be mentioned; and that the plan was adopted, not invented, by thofe who will have the hiftorical fame of it.

The Americans formed the outlines of their Conftitution, under the preffure of a calamitous war; it is not wonderful, therefore, they had not the refolution, fince exhibited by the French, to level all

provin-

CONSTITUTION of the AMERICAN STATES.

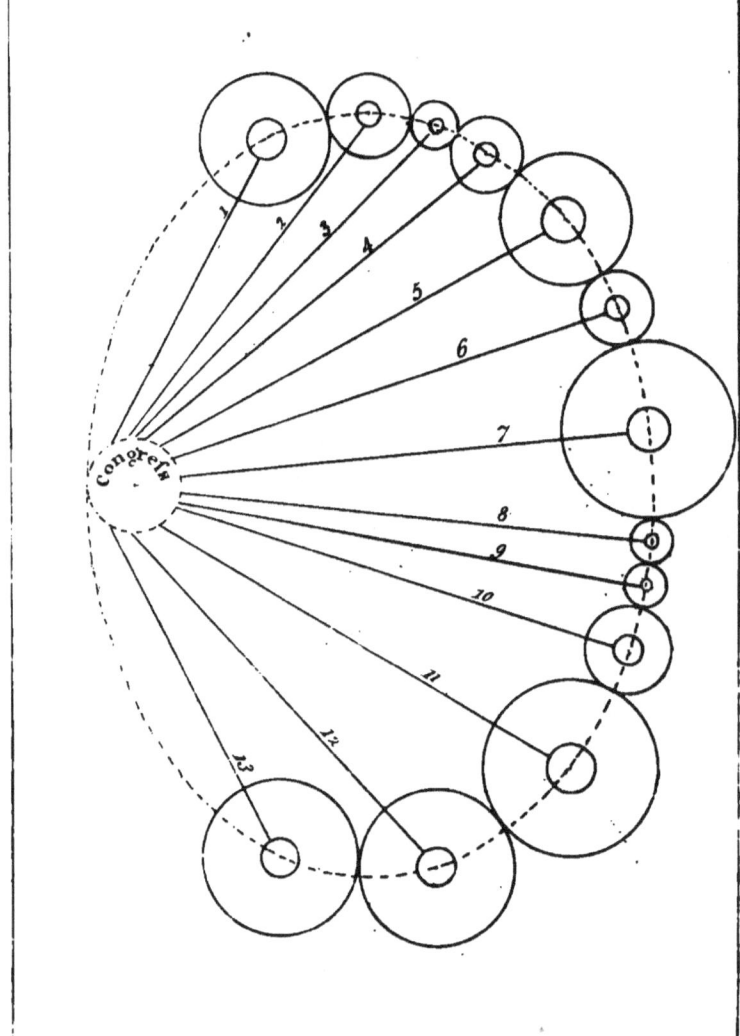

provincial diſtinctions, and to organize the whole nation into one body.

On a view of the annexed plate, your Royal Highneſs may diſcern, the unequal magnitudes of the bodies, which are connected with the central circle, and contribute a numerical proportion towards the wiſdom and power of congreſs.

1. New-Hampſhire.
2. Maſſachuſett.
3. Rhode Iſland.
4. Connecticut.
5. New-York.
6. New-Jerſey.
7. Pennſylvania.
8. Newcaſtle.
9. Kent and Suſſex.
11. Virginia.
12. North-Carolina.
13. South-Carolina.*

But each body has a diſtinct character, intereſt, and will; produced by the peculiarities of its in-

* See Votes of Congreſs in 1774. The form of the Republic has ſince been altered; but the alteration does not remedy the diſparity and provincial incongruities; which I conſider as the defects of the Conſtitution.

ternal

ternal organization: and the federative Constitution is a body, formed of thirteen complete bodies.

This is the defect of the American State; and not as Mr. Adams has afserted; the want of that balance by the counter-action of three powers, on which Montefquieu has taught him to imagine the liberties of Englifhmen depend.

The idea decorated by the ftyle of Montefquieu, is pretty; but it is groundlefs.

The three powers in England, are feldom, perhaps never balanced by counter-action. The Minifter of the day, by an opiate of infallible effect, deftroys their tendency to diverge, difagree, or oppofe each other.

If this were not the cafe, Liberty would not be the effect of three independent powers in any ftate. For two muft unite to govern the third; or corruption muft manage the whole.

The PUBLIC WILL is the only law of political liberty; and the PUBLIC FORCE, arifing from the organization of the whole nation, is its only fecurity. The head, the limbs, of fuch a body—its deliberative and executive powers—would have no occafion for the imaginary balances recommended by Montefquieu—

as the natural body is not affifted or improved by ftays, fteel-collars, and cork-rumps. Thefe are the indications and aids of deformity; which no real anatomift would recommend in the production or education of a vigorous, ufeful, and beautiful body.

But Mr. Adams has been Ambaffador in England; he drank at the fountain at St. James's: and he feems difpofed to convince his country (very *difinterefiedly* I muft fuppofe) that the evils occafioned by the Englifh Government, would not be evils in America; or that the prerogatives and privileges which in England render Liberty a tantalizing fhadow, an infulting name, would be bleffings in America, if conferred on the virtues of Adams, Hancock, and Lee; who will infure the tranfmiffion of them in their pofterity to the day of judgment.

But America will not attend to this antiquated fophiftry, whether decorated by the gaudy ornaments of a Burke; the curious patch-work of a Parr, to which all antiquity may have contributed its prettieft rags and tatters; or the homely, ungraceful garb which has been furnifhed her by Mr. John Adams.

The Americans are too well informed, not to

perceive they have wifely avoided the MYSTERY of the three powers. All the deviations from the English Government are improvements: and I exprefs my opinion of any defects in the American Conftitution, in a manner, I hope, perfectly confiftent with my real refpect for the talents and virtues which emancipated America.

The inconveniences of difparity and incongruity in the bodies to be united (not incorporated) were perceived, and fome provifion made for them in the proportionate delegations of every State to the general Congrefs. But I think the whole wants that unity, harmony, capacity of common judgment and general will, which would have refulted from a general organization of the republic into one body; and that in time, the various characters and interefts of the American States will difunite and alienate them.

The American Governments, feparately confidered, are improvements on the Government of England.

Their parliamentary reprefentations have more reality; their councils and governors have fewer pernicious privileges than the Nobles and Kings of Eng-

England; and the buds of induftry are not blighted by the difeafed breath of an indolent hierarchy. Security, liberty, and happinefs are more diffufed; and inftead of feeing a parifh ftarving in rags, while the Juftice of Peace, the Rector, and the Attorney are racking off at every joint the direful effects of gluttony and intemperance; every family is cloathed and fed comfortably; and health and happinefs are generally enjoyed.

When the French cabinet affifted in the emancipation of America, its object was merely to fever it from England, and to divide the empire of a rival power. It happily had not penetration to difcern all the confequences.

The partial liberty of the Englifh Prefs had been extremely ufeful to the American caufe; and the French were permitted to difcufs the queftions from which it originated, both in converfation and in their public writings. Government miftook the fubmiffion of France for a native and fixed torpor; and apprehended that flavery and fuperftition were the habits of Frenchmen, however they might chatter on Liberty and Science. The French auxiliaries returned from America fully charged with electric fire;

fire; difaffected Englifh affociated with Americans at Paris; and ftimulated philofophy to approach the ancient and mouldering fabric of defpotifm: the fparks of Liberty fell on touch-wood, and the whole at once blazed into afhes.

LESSON

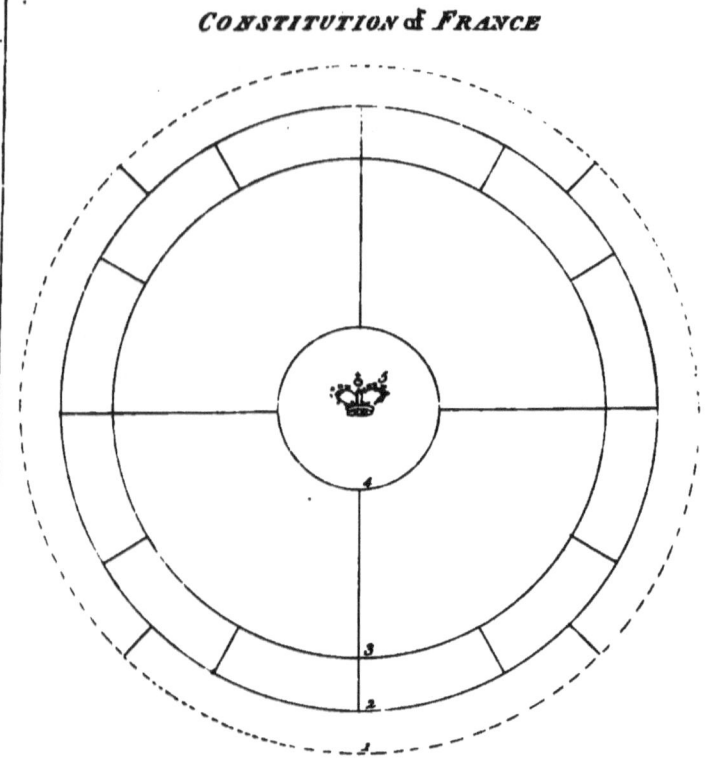

1. The People divided into Cantons but those who pay no Taxes & those who are in Servitude have no Votes & are not Citizens The Citizens in their Cantons chuse
2. The Electors by way of eminence divided into Districts. This Eminence or distinction arises from the privilege of electing the Judges, Magistrates, Bishops, &c. &c. who preside in
3. The Departments, The same Electors chuse
4. The National Assembly
5. The Executive Power having the Privilege of sending Commissioners to preside at the Assemblies of the Districts.

LESSON VIII.

CONSTITUTION OF FRANCE.

Sententia Platonis semper in ore fuit, " *Florere civitates, si Philo-*
" *sophi imperarent, aut Imperatores philosopharentur."*
Jul. Cap. in Marc. Aurel. §. 27.

Marcus Aurelius had always on his lips that sentence of Plato, " Communities would flourish, if philosophers ruled them, " or their rulers become philosophers."

I DO not mean to give in detail the external occurrences of the French Revolution: they are to be found in numerous publications; and they are accurately stated.

My intention is to delineate the object of the National Assembly, which is not understood in England, and is not clearly and permanently kept in view by the leading members of that respectable body.

Burke may declaim, " that a bloody and ferocious " democracy is demolishing ancient and venerable " institutions,"—the eye of philosophy will pass the

streights

ſtreights of Dover, and fix on the path of his ambition.—Stanhope may rummage conventicles for faints to hail an approaching millenium, *on the principles of the Engliſh Revolution!* when *Prieſtley* with the zeal and verboſity of a *Baxter*, and *Price* with the *meek* and *holy* ambition of *Praiſe-God Barebones*, may trample on the *Lauds*, the *Bonners*, the *Horſleys*, and the *Barringtons* of the time. Pitt may affect to rejoice in the improvements of a ſcience that would be fatal to the plauſibility of his impoſitions—and even Brand Hollis, emancipated from the puniſhment of detected bribery, may gratulate the immaculate purity of future Parliaments.—Theſe are the artifices of ſelf-intereſted empirics; who, like the fly in the fable, place themſelves on the wheel of human events, and buz to the ideots around them, that they influence and regulate its rotations.

The purpoſe of the National Aſſembly of France is—not to introduce a democracy in any ſenſe familiar to a mind ſo perverted by falſe philoſophy, ſuperſtition, and ſordid* ſelfiſhneſs, as that of Edmund

---

* The Prince will recollect the ſtipulations made by this frothy and ſentimental declaimer before he pronounced his oration on the regency.

Burke

Burke—it is not to imitate the measures of the English revolution, the political principles of which they despise—it is not to substitute Jansenism for Popery, Presbyterianism for Episcopacy, or to aid the pretended improvements of a system of imposition by the sophisms of Arians and Socinians—it is not to adopt the creeds of our political parties, or to justify the principles of Whigs or Tories—it is to abolish every contrivance and pretence by which one or a few may be privileged, first to benefit, then to injure millions—to destroy that principle of all modern governments, THAT A PART IS GREATER THAN THE WHOLE; and instead of applying a machine, denominated either Monarchic, Aristocratic, or Democratic, to govern the community for the advantage of individuals, orders, or professions—to organize the community itself; to form it into an actual body; to diffuse a lively and poignant sensibility over its surface; to connect the extremities with the seat of reflection and thought; and to introduce that general sympathy, which ever prevents a well-constructed body from injuring any of its parts.

Though this plan may have some novelty, the idea of it has been long suggested, and the general outlines given. His-

History will not enable us to judge of the whole of the views of Alfred: we learn, however, from the general traditions of Europe in his time, that ideas of a community were entertained superior to Kings or the Councils of Kings. In those assemblies of the Franks, from which the estates of France are denominated, they determined on peace or war, and examined the regulations which the King or Maire of the palace published. The ordonnances called capitularies had not the force of laws, were not enrolled in the Salic code, till sanctioned by the consent of the estates. The Assemblies consisted of *all* the free classes, or deputations from them; but the peasants were slaves.

The Mycle-gemot of Alfred was similar to those Assemblies. Modern Governments have avoided every thing analagous to them. In the original constitution of Geneva, periodical councils were provided with a compulsory power to oblige the magistrates and all the orders of the state to confine themselves within the prescribed bounds; but by the intrigues of the magistrates they were discontinued.

In the long and various struggles of the English Commons, before and since the celebrated Revolution

tion of 1688, they obtained no more than a pretended reprefentation for the ordinary purpofes of government, and the removal of fome abufes in the adminiftration of the laws.

Compared with other nations, the condition of an Englifhman was advantageous; but no man is free, whofe property and life are at the difcretion of others, in whofe appointment he has no real choice, and over whofe conduct he has no controul; and no man can be happy, while half the fruits of his induftry are forced from him to footh the pride and fofter the profligacy of numerous ufelefs and oppreffive orders.

At the acceffion of the Houfe of Hanover, the pretended reprefentation, called an Englifh Parliament, was appointed, by thofe who had the power, for three years. To prove that the public was nothing, even while it was proclaimed through Europe the *Nation* had made choice of your Royal Highnefs's family, George the Firft had been but a few years on the throne, when it had the profligate audacity to render three years feven, and to enact this violation of faith and right the future law of Parliament. The Roman Decemvirate, or college

lege of ten, is juſtly conſigned to perpetual infamy for acting on a ſimilar principle with the Engliſh Houſe of Commons; being eſtabliſhed for a limited time, for a ſpecific purpoſe, and attempting to turn a temporary truſt into perpetual tyranny.

He who commits a truſt, parts only with the *adminiſtration*; it is not poſſible to convert a truſt into an abſolute right, or into a diſcretionary and independent power.

The Engliſh Parliament, intoxicated with ſucceſs, avowed a doctrine deſtructive of the firſt principles of free governments: it was declared, the people when aſſembled (and they never were aſſembled) were every thing: when they had made their election, they were nothing; and Parliament became *omnipotent*. Though the ſupreme power in every community, formed to be free, muſt be indiviſible and inalienate; though it be impoſſible it ſhould ſubmit its ſovereignty to an Emperor, a King, or a Senate, without violating the act by which it exiſts as a community, without annihilating itſelf—and out of nothing, nothing can ariſe—yet Parliament maintained that its power and prerogatives were paramount, diſcretionary, and incontrolable, not only

only over the persons from whom it pretended a delegation, but over those provinces and colonies which were not included in the farce of representation.

The despotic violence with which every thing was conducted in the proposed subjugation of America— the political maxims avowed, and the sanguine measures executed, roused the attention of the world.

England saw itself, as well as its dependencies, trampled with impunity, by pretended delegates assuming the prerogatives of despotic masters. Petitions and remonstrances were presented, and associations formed, to induce the monster to moderate its ravages, and to prevail on Parliament *to reform itself*.

The pusillanimity and absurdity of those measures, in a powerful community pretending to be free, gave rise to a pamphlet, entitled, LETTERS ON POLITICAL LIBERTY, addressed to the Associations; that pamphlet first drew my attention to the possible mode of *organizing* a community into a free, active, and powerful body; having and retaining a permanent judgment and will; and exercising those powers, without tumult or disorder, over all its delegations,

legations, whether Kings, Senates, or Magistrates.* The Author calls on the nation, in a tone of earnest enthusiasm, to restore the constitution of Alfred with such improvements as suit the present condition of personal liberty: and by these means, to remove the numerous evils of the police, and the gross abuses of legislative authority.—The Associations were astonished, but not advised. A translation was circulated in France with great rapidity; and it was at Paris, when the translator of that pamphlet was sent into the Bastile—I formed, in company with —————— my opinions on the constitution of a free state. I found the philosophers of France better instructed in the subject than those of England; †

---

* A similar pamphlet was published about the same time, and containing similar ideas, called A Plan of Association on Constitutional Principles; and I suspect by the language, it was written by the same Author.

† I except a Gentleman who has dedicated works to your Royal Highness in the plain and manly language of Virtue. In Lectures on Political Principles, by David Williams, ideas of organized constitutions suited to all climates, &c. are opposed to those of Montesquieu with great address and effect. But the Author, bold as he is, expresses himself in the language of speculation, little imagining that the National Assembly of France would immediately publish so glorious a Commentary on his work.

but

but they had no apprehenfion, that the general difpofition of the French nation would admit of their ideas and wifhes.

When the diftrefs of the treafury threatened a bankruptcy, and Necker advifed the provincial affemblies and the meeting of the Notables, he had no intention to form a free conftitution: his object was fimilar to that of the Kings of England, who fummoned the deputies of boroughs to devife modes of conveying their contributions without trouble. Necker was not aware, that the fatires of Voltaire on the Clergy had rendered them juftly and univerfally odious; that the numerous and oppreffive privileges of the Nobles were deeply, though filently refented; and that France abounded with philofophers, who would promptly feize the firft occafion to develope and execute their political ideas.—This occafion arofe, and the conftitution of France was imagined.

It is hardly fair to offer a delineation of a fabric not yet formed; some parts of which may not be determined upon, and some may be altered. But if this little work should ever be honoured with any attention in France, I hope my purpose will not be misunderstood. Though I do not join in any of those compliments to the National Assembly, which are sent from this country, to assist private views, and to give consequence to interested parties—the designs and efforts of real patriotism in France have not a warmer friend in the world than myself: and if I offer remarks on an event the most beneficial to humanity in all the records of mankind, it is to afford assistance and to induce the philosophic politicians of the National Assembly to re-consider their fundamental laws.

In the definition and appointment of citizens, there is a want of justice; and in the construction of a political state, as in that of a private character,

" Want of Virtue is want of sense."

The first and general purpose of society is to guard the weak against the strong, and the poor against the rich.

rich. The first division of all the people of France is into cantons; but in voting for the next rank of citizens called Electors, those who do not pay a certain sum towards the public expence are excluded: i. e. they are enslaved.

The burthen of labour and of military service, is on the poor, and if philosophy had produced its full effect in the National Assembly, we should have had this reproach of political Constitutions removed. For she, like

The genuine muse removes the thin disguise,
 That cheats the world, whene'er she deigns to sing,
And full as meritorious to her eyes
 Seems the poor soldier as the mighty King.

In the present Constitution of France the most helpless of the people are deprived of the only consolation or ground of hope, the only stimulus to content, honesty, and virtue in their situation—*the choice of their masters.* It is this condemnation to a species of slavery, that renders servants a separate and profligate corps; and a similar injustice to those of the people, whose poverty is a sufficient evil, will be a disease in the constitution, which no palliatives can remove.

The Assemblies in the Cantons are too numerous. Montesquieu (Let. Pers.) observes, " The heads of " the greatest men seem to be narrowed (retrecies) " when they are assembled; and in the greatest *number* of wise men, there is the least wisdom."

Alfred was aware of this truth; and the first divisions of his political body, like the capillary vessels on the surface of the natural, were small, and formed to execute their offices without violence. The tithings consisted only of ten families. I never saw an assembly, exceeding twenty, whatever the abilities of the members, that was not more disposed to passion and tumult, than to reason and judgment.

The distinction of the ELECTORS in the districts, and the privilege of electing both into the departments and into the National Assembly, is without reason.—The graduated elections are not so equitable, or so well imagined, as those in the Constitution of Alfred.

The National Assembly, if chosen in the departments, would be every thing designed by Alfred in the institution of the Mycle-gemot; but if its number could be reduced, and business done more by open committees and printed propositions, than by oratory, it would be improved. It should also openly and decidedly avow its competency to form and enact all constitutional and fundamental laws without any permission of the executive power. A period should be as fixed as the constitution, in which a similar assembly might always be chosen, and meet without summons or leave from any other power; and its business should be, to revise and correct all fundamental regulations, to inspect the conduct of the ordinary government and legislation, and to redress or remove all national grievances.

The interference of the executive power by commissioners in the districts is a privilege of fatal effect; and if not withdrawn, will soon render the constitution of France as corrupt, as vicious, and as much a deception, as the pretended of England.

THIS account of the French Conſtitution, in the firſt Edition, has been thought too conciſe to remove prejudice or to inſtruct ignorance in the people of this country.

They who have made this juſt remark, ſhould recollect, the Leſſons were immediately addreſſed to an informed though a young and diſſipated perſonage, and that it did not occur even to the vanity of the author, they would be rapidly circulated through the nation.

To remove the objection, it will be neceſſary to explain the terms MYCLE-GEMOT and WITTENA-GEMOT in the Conſtitution of Alfred: the firſt meaning the Folk-mot or Great Aſſembly of the Nation by its deputies, which he intended ſhould ever meet annually on Saliſbury plain, to reviſe and adjudge the acts of the executive power, and of the legiſlature called the WITTENAGEMOT, or the Aſſembly of Wiſe-men, analogous to the French idea of notables.*

When

---

* See numerous authorities for this opinion in Bede, Spelman, Selden, Wilkins, Wright, Letters on Political Liberty; and a very excellent little work on Saxon Inſtitutions by the
late

When the measures of the King and his Great Council, his Wittenagemot, or Notables, were deemed conducive to the public welfare, they were sanctioned as the permanent laws of the land. When adjudged otherwise, they were forbidden and abrogated.

The anarchy, from Danish violence and depredation, nearly obliterated these wise and admirable institutions: and William the Conqueror, while his prudence suggested the expedience of not exasperating the nation by wholly renouncing them, was induced by a sagacious spirit of despotism, to prefer the Wittenagemot to the Folk-mot or Mycle-gemot; as the former was manageable by his power or his wealth; the latter must have restrained him within the limits of useful laws, and measures of obvious national advantage.

The English Parliament is the offspring of the Wittenagemot, the choice of the Conqueror, with

---

late Dr. Squire, Bishop of St. David: who seems to have renounced the Spirit of his order, and like the present Bishop D'Autun, to have sunk all episcopal properties in the enlarged views of a good citizen and the humane qualities of an amiable man.

some

some supposed advantages from the addition of the House of Commons: but still retaining its original character respecting the crown; and perpetually exemplifying in its extravagant pretensions and exceptionable conduct, the necessity of national revision, controul and correction in such an annual deputation as the Folk-mot.

When the necessities of the French King rendered expedient some kind of application to the nation, its antient records were examined; and a spirit, analogous to that of the Norman, induced him to call the Notables, the Wittenagemot, not a representation of the country, or any thing similar to the Mycle-gemot.——But the institution of the Provincial Assemblies was an *error of Necker's, most fortunate to the French nation*; it was making apertures in the great dykes of arbitrary power; and when the waters burst their bounds, they soon became irresistible.

Whether the great extent and population of France, or the documents of the antient institutions of the Franks, or the suggestions of any late speculations, induced the French Reformers to adopt a
plan

plan similar to that of Alfred, I am not qualified to determine.

They have in some degree, though not fully, adopted his idea of deputations of deputations, which are absolutely necessary to render the actual representation of populous and extensive kingdoms consistent with their industry and peace.

They have also appointed all choice and election to be by divisions of the people; to originate in the lower class; and to proceed upwards. This is essential to liberty.

But they have differed from Alfred; and where they have differed, I think they have erred.

To have attempted abolishing slavery or the power of the church, would probably have involved Alfred in ruin. But every freeman, without exception, was an elector. This is not the case in France. And I object to the exclusion of those who are unable to pay a small rate or tax, not in the spirit of criticism, but from a conviction of injustice and impolicy, in depressing mere incapacity, stigmatizing the unfortunate, giving additional power to the possession of property, which in itself is power—while all the genuine principles and regulations of justice, are wholly directed against the injurious exertions of power or force.

The first divisions of the people are into cantons; and their first voting Assemblies consist of six or seven hundred. These are multitudes, incapable of judgment or choice, whatever the character of the individuals may be: and for this opinion, I appeal to the experience of the world. For not a single Assembly has existed, as an exception. What then is to be expected but passion or disorder from such mingled multitudes of French peasants? Alfred perceived this truth: and his first Assemblies consisted only of ten housholders.

The French Reformers, as if sensible of their error in the first division, attempt to remedy it by another; which I am truly sorry to consider as the commission of another injury.—The cantons elect into the districts: and the electors in the districts are formed into a numerous extensive aristocracy. For they are denominated, by way of eminence, the *Electors*; they chuse into the departments, into the rectories, bishoprics, the various offices of magistracy, and even into the National Assembly.

This, besides being an injustice to the electors in
the

the cantons below and the departments above, is facilitating the future intrigues of the executive power by directing them to a particular spot. And to insure the mischief, they have committed to the King the nomination of commissioners to preside in the elections.

The National Assembly first met at Versailles to assist the King to provide for the public exigencies: and to devise, in conjunction with him, such regulations as would prevent similar evils.—It therefore assembled as a Wittenagemot, or an English Parliament, for specified purposes and with limited powers. But when a few incidents had shaken to the dust the remains of ancient despotism, the Assembly gradually changed its tone; and from being a municipal, legislative Commission, like the British Legislature, it assumed Constitutional Powers, and became analogous to the Mycle-gemot of Alfred.

In this new character, the Assembly has acted with a prudence verging on timidity, and sometimes descending to equivocation.

The Mycle-gemot of Alfred was in effect the Nation: it was open to every freeman who had a complaint against the government: and the members

bers at a signal could have produced the nation in arms on Salisbury Plain. That possibility was the firm basis of its constitutional influence over the executive and legislative powers; and the knowledge of it rendered its exercise always unnecessary: it was like the influence of the whole body over its limbs, the source of order and general harmony, never of disagreement or confusion.

When the National Assembly assumed new powers and a new character, when it appeared as the Myclegemot of Alfred, a Constitutional Assembly to decree fundamental laws, and to assign the provinces of executive, legislative, and municipal authority; there was just as much reason in their consulting the King and requiring his sanction; as in consulting the future magistrates of the projected municipalities.

The members of the National Assembly often insinuate that future legislatures will not have their powers; but will they not, like the English Parliament, assume them? And are not the strongest hopes of a Counter-Revolution founded, on the probability that a future Assembly may repeal the acts of the present.

To

To prevent this evil, the National Assembly should separate its constitutional from its legislative acts. In the former, the executive power should never be consulted. The mode of chusing the ordinary legislature should be distinguished from that of appointing the National Assembly, which should be elected annually, and meet on a certain day, like the Mycle-gemot of Alfred, to signify the national approbation or disapprobation of the proceedings of Government and acts of the legislature, and to revise, correct, and improve all constitutional regulations or fundamental laws.

LESSON

LESSON IX.

PRINCIPLES OF LEGISLATION.

———*Suadere Principi quod oporteat, multi laboris; affentatio erga Principem quemcumque fine affectu peragitur.*
                                                                    Tac.

It is difficult to advife Princes—it is not difficult to flatter them.

Acquiescing in the fentiment of Tacitus, I fhall not long detain your Royal Highnefs on the ufe to be made of the information I have taken the liberty to lay before you.

An attentive view of the political conftitutions I have delineated, will convince your Royal Highnefs, that the principles of legiflation and government are ftudied; and that political and ecclefiaftical impoftures will be generally detected and deftroyed.

The difference of the French and Englifh Nation will be, that of an organized body acting for itfelf,
                                                                    and

and a paffive mafs acted upon : I need not point out the advantage to France, befides that of its climate and population.

But as this may be a truth of magnitude, not to be readily admitted, your Royal Highnefs will permit me to fuggeft the immediate effect of emigration from caufes which you fhould be anxious to remove, if you regard the future population and ftate of the country.

The conftruction of the French government implies a perfect police; for the magiftrates are *chofen* in all the neighbourhoods, and their offices are annual: indeed the whole body guards and protects itfelf. This will be foon known to thofe prodigious multitudes of timid and female houfholders in England, who are plundered by every device that avarice can fuggeft, to thofe appointed to protect them.

Perfect liberty of opinion, both in thought and words, will carry over confcientious and induftrious diffenters, who are here fubject to difadvantages, from circumftances which do them honour. To prevent the confequences of this evil, I do not mean that Puritanifm fhould be fubftituted for the
efta-

established rites; but that the government is unjust, when it engages in one religious faction to the inconvenience of another; and that, by avoiding this error, France will draw from England great numbers of its useful citizens.*

I will not weary your Royal Highness by a minute detail of the disadvantages under which England must act, if its government be not improved, in proportion as France advances in the judicious construction of its political constitution.

Your Royal Highness will recollect, that the English Government is a machine acting on the people, and managed at the will and for the interest of

---

* Princes and Magistrates should scorn to be apparitors to ambitious, selfish, and useless priests, or the ministers of their intolerant and cruel purposes. Darius hearing of disputes in Persia, of similar importance with those which now agitate the superstitious world, asked the Greeks, what sums they would take to eat their parents? They exclaimed, Not all the gold in the world. He asked the Callattii, a people inhabiting a part of India, and who eat their parents, what they would take to burn them? The proposal produced cries of horror.——Go to your habitations, said the King; and eat or not eat your parents as you like; *but do not molest each other.* The *Priests of both parties* murmured at the *last* injunction.

parti-

particular orders; whereas the CONSTITUTION OF A COUNTRY, to bear even a definition, should comprehend the people; to produce Liberty, it should allow them a choice of the Legislature and Magistrates.

When that choice is made, a power should remain in the community by the appointment of a periodical assembly, to prevent all abuses of trust; and all interference, of the ordinary or municipal legislature, in fundamental laws.

The Mycle-gemot of Alfred and the National Assembly of France are calculated for this purpose; their objects are constitutional: but we have no assembly in England bearing the slightest analogy to them. Hence the absurdities perpetually recurring in English legislation; the power of making laws for temporary purposes confounded with the national sovereignty; and the most iniquitous usurpations justified by assimilating the ideas of trust and right: infamous and audacious adventurers, the tools of feudal despots, of mercantile companies, and corrupt ministers, in marketable boroughs, holding the language of masters to six millions of people; and con-

contending for the lucrative privilege of defpoiling them.*

The laws, when made, would be equitably and expeditioufly adminiftered, by judges and magiftrates chofen and approved by the vicinages; and the periodical vifitations of loquacious and unprincipled lawyers, would not act on the country as periodical peftilences.†

The juftices of the peace, the moft numerous and important magiftrates, would not be, as they now are, the devoted inftruments of devoted inftruments. And the Clergy, emancipated from an humiliating and difhonourable patronage, which muft ever have an intereft in exalting fycophants and depreffing

---

* During the late illnefs of the King, minifterial majorities in a temporary legiflature claimed the abfolute fovereignty of the ftate.

† The practice of attornies, called pettifoggers, is to inftruct evidence in fafe and fuccefsful modes of perjury. The council are often in collufion with thefe attornies; they favour their prepared evidences, and abufe thofe who are unprepared, with a degree of profligate impudence and unprincipled villainy, which the judges fhould correct with more determined feverity, if they wifh, as they certainly muft, to preferve reverence for the laws, and refpect for thofe who adminifter them.

manly

manly and useful talents, would assume a new character, and from being the tools of corrupt influence, would become the real ministers of religion and virtue.

Improvements of this kind *must* take place, if the Constitution of France be established, or this Country will immediately lose its rank.

Though I do not subscribe to the opinion of your Royal Father, that the measures at Paris have a tendency to deprive Europe of its Kings in thirty years, I am sure that in a very few, they will render the duty and office of a King of England different from that of a splendid partisan, directing the servility and avarice of ranks, classes, and professions to private purposes; encountering faction by faction; involving himself in the inextricable labyrinth of ineffectual expedients. If you keep your eye on the constitution of France, you may prepare yourself for the character you may have to sustain: and if you favour the necessary improvements of the government of your country, you will secure its just rank among the nations of Europe, fix your own happiness on a certain foundation, and en-
roll

roll your name among the great benefactors of mankind.

These are wishes which will never be expressed in your hearing, by the parasites of your Court, or the objects of your political confidence. I have no private interest in the trouble I have taken. I feel no ambition to be the competitor of your favorites. I have no desire that a moment of my peace should depend, even on a Prince, who can, one day, take pains to engage and captivate; induce generous youth to enlist under his banners and wear his uniform; and the next, not recollect or know them. I seek not your favour, Sir—and, in the decent and legal exercise of my abilities, I respectfully presume I need not fear your displeasure. In all the imaginable fluctuations of parties, my name will never be brought to your Royal Highness in the lists of candidates for places. And in the temporary confusion and anarchy of any possible revolution, my age, my infirmities, my inclinations, and my habits, preclude all effort and hope for my own advantage.

If, therefore, in the hints I have ventured to submit to you, I have erred—the fault is in my judgment, not in my heart: if I have suggested any
thing

thing that may influence your mind, the benefit will be—not to me, but to your Royal Highnefs and to your Country.

LESSON X.

ON THE MODE OF STUDYING AND PROFITING

BY

MR. BURKE'S REFLECTIONS

ON THE

LATE REVOLUTION IN FRANCE.

'Η γὰρ τῶν λόγων κρίσις πολλῆς ἐςι πείρας τελευταιον ἐπιγέννημα.
For criticism, or an ability to judge of writings, is the last child of long experience.   Longinus, 17.

THIS is my apology for presuming to point out to your Royal Highness, the important sublimities, and captivating beauties of a great work; destined by the Author, to check the progress of democratic licence, and impious infidelity, and to restore the original and sacred principles, on which the Governments of Europe were first established.

On the first view of a performance, so inimical

to those rights for which I have pleaded, and those principles I have attempted to establish, in the preceding Lessons, I was inclined to dispute the positions of the writer.

I had been accustomed to think eloquence inferior to wisdom—' Aaron shall be thy speaker; and thou ' shalt be to him as God.'—I thought I had perceived a material distinction, between profound inquiry, and the art of popular persuasion—the former, the object of the highest, the best philosophy, I considered as forming the noblest characters in human nature: and I deemed the position of Plato, ' that an Orator should be a Philosopher,' as the mere homage of Poetry and Eloquence at the shrine of wisdom. Human life is too short, to unite the accomplishments of the two characters. Cicero attempted it: but Cicero in philosophy, was merely a man of knowledge. Who could combine, the profound thought of a Montesquieu with the talents of a Chatham or a Mansfield? I had considered the melioration of Gothic systems, and the laws and customs which have been lately supposed to produce public happiness, as owing—not to natural historians, or experimental philosophers; not to poetry, painting, mufic, or oratory; not to arithmetic, mathematics, or even the difcoveries of Newton—but to the works of fuch men as Sidney, Harrington, Locke, Montefquieu, Steuart, and Smith: and I thought it a duty to defend the philofophy they had profeffed from the verbofe fcurrilities of a popular writer.

But on the perufal of Mr. Burke's ' wonderful' Letter, your Royal Highnefs will perceive I have been miftaken; you will judge that wifdom fhould give place to eloquence; that ' the wife in heart ' fhall be called prudent, but the fweet in tongue ' fhall find greater things.'

I was alfo deterred by the information, that a competitor in the fame art had feen the letter of Mr. Burke, fome months before its publication, and was preparing an anfwer.

A contention of practifed prize-fighters would irrefiftibly attract the literary rabble; and the gentle voice of reafon, would not be heard.

But having mentioned Mr. Burke, in a former Leffon, with epithets of difapprobation and reproach; and having imbibed from his work that principle of exquifite fentiment and fine feeling which alternately with religion is the substitute of honour and virtue, I find it my duty to exhibit his character on the best, viz. on his own authority

To serve the double purpose of relieving my 'penitent sensibility'—and to familiarise your Royal Highness with the principles of criticism, I hope to impress on your mind, that a knowledge of the author is necessary to that of his work; and that you should take it from himself, for this indisputable reason, " that every man must know his own cha-" racter."

Great critics resemble their authors. Longinus delineates the beauties of Homer, in passages equally beautiful—I, therefore, view Mr. Burke, not as the morning star, dropping gentle and beneficent dew; not as a regular planet, in that wonderful system, the daily blessings of which we participate; but a blazing eccentric comet, of mystic and menacing omen, and my eye is led to survey it from the tail.

In the last page of his " divine rhapsody" he thus describes himself—and your Royal Highness is intreated to observe, the exemplary modesty of so great a man. When public objects fill his " disin-" terested" mind, it soars like an infernal fury, and

scat-

scatters vengeance and misery over " disobedient" nations—when he retires within himself, we discern only the humility of a Christian, and a gentleness and bashfulness truly sentimental.

" I," the great man says, " have little to recom-
" mend my opinions, but long observation and
" much impartiality." My Lord Mansfield, who still possesses his mental faculties in great vigor, pronounces the French Revolution, an event in history totally new, to which no former facts and incidents can apply. Here is, long observation against long observation: but I shall presently state the circumstance which may induce Mr. Burke to give the preference to himself. On the subject of his " im-
" partiality" there can be no doubt. Has any man conversed with, or heard this orator, and supposed him capable of harbouring prejudice?

" They come from one who has been no tool of
" power, no flatterer of greatness, and who, in his
" last acts, does not wish to belye the tenour of his
" life."

It must give your Royal Highness pleasure, to learn from the authority of this great man himself, that the opinion of his implicit devotion to a late Marquis,

for

for good and substantial considerations, is groundless; that he purchased his villa and estate at Beaconsfield with the accumulations of his own patrimony; that he represents a borough in parliament, by the free uninfluenced election of the burgesses; and, though while in office, he offered incense of adoration at the shrine of royalty, he conscientiously balanced it out of office, by pronouncing on the melancholy and afflicting indisposition of your Royal Father, " that the Almighty had hurled him from his " throne." He remarks on the proceedings of the Revolution Society, " that the misfortunes of Kings " make a delicious repast to some sort of palates"— The repast suits not the palate of Mr. Burke, unless it be stimulated by disappointment, or by some strong obstacle to the attainment of his wishes. This, I am sure, your Royal Highness will think a sufficient cause, and to use his own phrase, not to belye the tenour of his life.

" They come from one, almost the whole of
" whose public life has been a struggle for the li-
" berty of others; from one, in whose breast no an-
" ger durable or vehement has ever been kindled,
" but by what he considers as tyranny; and who
" snatches

" snatches from his share in the endeavours which
" are used by good men to discredit opulent oppres-
" sion, the hours he has employed on your affairs;
" and who in so doing persuades himself he has not
" departed from his usual office."

Your Royal Highness will here admire the modest address with which the great orator mingles, the distinguished parts he has acted, in opposition to the American war, and in the Impeachment of Mr. Hastings. To place these great actions in a true light, your Royal Highness must be informed that the Declaratory Bill, the very brand which set America on fire, was fabricated in councils of which this orator participated. But you will take with you, the moment Mr. Burke was dismissed, he became a determined opponent to the Minister, and the war he conducted; he execrated him as a traitor to the constitution; and pledged his honour and character to impeach him. When events indicated the advantage of a coalition with that minister, the wonderful placability of our Author's nature was displayed. He passed instantly from mortal hatred to the most enthusiastic friendship, and from bitter reproach to sublime panegyric. I am sensible, if such apparent contradiction

tradiction and such dereliction of all principle, were fairly chargeable on a philosopher, Mr. Burke would annex to his name the most infamous epithets. But a Christian: a believer of those doctrines which so amicably blend high church tories with the votaries of the church of Rome, has advantages which moralists cannot enjoy. By rites, ceremonies, and external atonements, conscience may be set, on a pivot, like a weather-vane, to turn with the airy current of self-interest.

I would impress these hints the more carefully on your Royal Highness, as I understand the alternate councils of Cumberland and the little White house (on the late re-establishment of which I congratulate your Royal Highness) discover a reluctance and timidity respecting this admirable and expedient religion. If any future event should give the power, I should advise its avowal; and if the sacred bench would admit of a preaching prelate, that Mr. Burke be seated on it, reserving an annual portion of every parliamentary season for the impeachment.

In the prosecution of Mr. Hastings, the conduct of this great and good man is equally admirable with his opposition to the American war. The House

House of Commons stated a certain number of propositions, referring to acts which, in Mr. Hastings were or were not, violations of law, or violations of a specified trust. But of what advantage would determinations on such questions have been to the learning of the country. The history and antiquities of Hindustan; the various politics of its states; its ancient, complex, and extensive mythology; the doctrines, rites, and ceremonies of its religion; its population, ranks, casts, customs, and manners; have been minutely detailed—and the wisdom and knowledge of ages have been compressed into a morning entertainment; have been arranged into speeches, which have contributed greatly to the improvement of the attending audience; and, by the industry and panegyrics of newspaper reporters have been diffused through the nation to its great advantage.

The placability and mercy of our author, appears in this transaction, but with the more dignity, as every object is magnified by foggy interpositions.

While the menaces of virtue, personated by Mr. Burke, hung over the head of Hastings, a confidential friend and associate orator, carried a White Flag,

to

to the agent of the offender; but whether from all the enemies to Indian oppression, which he here calls " good men"—whether to avert the impending storm, or generously to enable the sufferer to prepare for it — we can only conjecture — the agent, being naturally a Marplot, having fully answered the main question, when a previous hint had only been given.

Charity, however, will incline us to suppose, that the generosity, almost supernatural, which erased from the author's mind, all the resentment, rage, and abhorrence, excited by the conduct of Lord North; and introduced the gentle passions of forgiveness and friendship; would not have been, and will not yet be, absolutely and eternally implacable to Mr. Hastings; though, in intercourses of chicane and corruption with Begums, Nabobs, and Rajahs, he may have forgotten the laws of his country, or violated the universal maxims of virtue.

In respect to France, a similar disposition to placability is discoverable even in the highest paroxysm of the author's rage. For after warming his imagination into frenzy on the royal sufferings; and execrating the National Assembly, the philosophers,

the

the jacobins, and all the real and imaginary caufes of the facrilegious difhonor; he admits a poffibility that royalty might devife or commit acts that would require examination and inquiry. Here is a fair opening for reconciliation between the offending people of France and this great orator. Let the National Affembly *vote an Impeachment:* and if they give Mr. Burke the management, they may be affured, not only of his forgivenefs and friendfhip, but that the King and Queen will be difpofed of for life. What a glorious fate! What a characteriftic appointment! All Europe would be occupied on his orations, and filled with his fame: and when Providence calls him—it is hoped very late—from the trophies of his virtues and duty here; his future reward, to give effect to the cultivation of his prefent talents, we may humbly fuppofe, will be—To IMPEACH THE DEVIL TO ALL ETERNITY!

The 'good' man proceeds—" They come from " one who defires honors, diftinctions, and emolu-" ments, but little; and who expects them not at " all."

The advantage of religion is in nothing fo great, as in veiling fecret infirmities or crimes. It is true, the

the eye of God is supposed to penetrate all disguise and all darkness; but his ministers are placable, and every thing has its price. Mr. Burke was *the only* partisan who stipulated with the Pall-Mall Cabal, previous to an oration on the Regency which unnecessarily precipitated your Royal Highness into unpopularity. How many of the Burkes were to be provided for; and how Indian peculation might be reconciled to virtue and humanity in that holy family, ' I will not tell in Gath or publish in the ' streets of Askalon, lest the ungodly should blas- ' pheme:' Dr. Parr would have been endued with the faculty of consecrating the transaction, and guarding it from the scoffs of " atheistic" patriotism or of profligate impertinence.

It must be expected, an orator " has no contempt" of fame, " but Mr. Burke" never sacrificed his interest to it: and he " has no fear of obloquy," though he has prosecuted newspapers, and expressed apprehension, and alarm, at paragraphists, in a manner that would be deemed pusillanimous in an Abbess of King's Place. But it is to be observed that Mr. Burke trembles only for the cause of liberty and humanity, for the sacred and august fabric

bric of government, which is to be forcibly entered only by his party, and then to be eternally preserved from profanation and ruin.

The Speaker of the House of Commons will attest, that " he shuns contention, though he will " hazard an opinion"——That " he wishes to pre-" serve consistency," the world is disposed to doubt; not knowing that " he would preserve con-" sistency, by varying his means to secure the " unity of his end, and that when the *equipoise* of " the vessel in which he sails may be endangered by " overloading it upon one side, he is desirous of " carrying the small weight of his reasons to that " *which may preserve its equipoise.*"

Your Royal Highness will regret with me, that even so beautiful a sentence should conclude the account the great orator condescends to give of himself. It alludes to the condition of a passenger on the river Thames, where the difference in the various contents of his pockets obliges him to shift and change positions; and it furnishes an exact image of Mr. Burke's life.

The modesty of the author would not permit him to hint at the exertion of mind which produced this

great

great work. His mighty brain teemed with it, nearly twelve months—I wish I could fully devote as many days, to render your Royal Highness sensible of all its merits.

That any man, not educated an inquisitor, and not long accustomed to derive his pleasure from torture and misery, should be able to turn his eye with malignant aversion on four and twenty millions of his fellow-creatures, suddenly emancipated from oppressive tyranny, and anxiously seeking their future security in the deliberations of reason and the provisions of prudent humanity—would be improbable in theory. It would be incredible, that a civilized citizen; participating the blessings of freedom under a mild government; cultivating letters and pretending to philosophy—should, without distraction and frenzy, harbour a whole year in his mind, ideas so horrible, wishes so diabolical, as are expressed in almost every page of this work. But the operations of self-interest, sublimed by religion,* produce miracles.

* The reader is to observe, that the Author uses the word Religion, as signifying the varied superstition which governments employ to impoverish and enslave the people.

I   Mr.

Mr. Burke wrote his " wonderful" Letter, immediately on receiving the sanction of the Minister* to his sentiments in Parliament. As events fluctuated in France, the production was corrected, and the author has been alternately agitated and tortured by hope and despondence, " that the evils of " the revolution might or might not justify his opi-' " nions." At last, the Aristocratic Oracle gave the signal. Calonne announced the plan of a counter-revolution. Burke put on his magic spectacles, distinctly saw, the Austrians marching through Flanders, the Spaniards in the Pyrennees, the Savoyards and Swifs in the Alps, and German and English officers sneaking off singly and reluctantly from poverty in England to assist in the projected massacre and devastation. Burke grew frantic with joy: he snuffed

---

* Common minds should cautiously pronounce concerning Ministers who are born Statesmen, or Heaven-born: but it is certain Mr. Pitt's approbation of Mr. Burke's speech on the French Revolution occasioned all those measures of France, which embarrassed his Spanish negociation.

The National Assembly had been instructed from England, to distinguish the wishes of the English Administration from those of the Nation: the measures of France would otherwise have been more decisive, and a War must have ensued.

the

the murky air, loaded with the exhalations of twenty millions of atheiſtic and patriotic carcaſes. "The "incenſe is divine!" exclaimed the "holy" man—"My prophecies and revelations ſhall be honoured;" and lo—the Book was publiſhed.

When your Royal Highneſs is, thus, in poſſeſſion of the author's character and motives, you may eaſily judge of his work.

I have intimated, in a previous leſſon, the principal cauſes of the French Revolution. When the fortreſs of deſpotiſm was carried; the victors were not content with ſtipulations to prevent future annoyance, they razed it to the ground, and projected a new and uſeful ſtructure.

The genius of England, in political deſign, had been ſo long the theme of panegyric, that it was not imagined, the French would preſume to attempt any thing beyond an humble imitation of the Engliſh Government. Your Royal Highneſs will judge of the feelings of "mere Engliſhmen," by thoſe which actuate Mr. Burke, when it was underſtood, they projected a new conſtitution, and meant to claim the merit of originality.

In the "Revelations" of the author your Royal High-

Highness may be instructed, to consider this presumption as a "national insult," and a cause of war as justifiable as any that has determined our cabinets.

But if it should not rouze that NATIONAL HATRED, which political fraud and pious artifice have assiduously generated and preserved—the dangers of the example furnished by France, are extremely numerous and alarming, to those who occupy (disinterestedly without doubt) the various departments of our " wonderful constitution;" which is peculiarly " excellent" *in its faults; produces equality by the common and necessary causes of inequality, and confers benefits and blessings by injustice and injury.*

Whence are derived these mystic advantages?— Your Royal Highness will perceive, in a former Lesson, I traced the genuine principles of English Liberty, in Saxon institutions: but the Saxons being heathens, consequently atheists or philosophers, according to our author's learned and liberal use of the terms, I took liberties with their rude sketches, and endeavoured to form into elements the principles that have immortalized the name of Alfred.* In

---

* The Author has been informed, the political Diagrams of these Lessons are used, by intelligent parents, to give ideas of political

In thefe—there is an evident diftinction of GOVERNMENT and SOVEREIGNTY. Government has the power of municipal legiflation, and its laws are obligatory on individuals, corporate bodies, &c.—the nation arranged, organifed, and acting as fovereign, has conftitutional authority over the power of government.

The firft law, in this fpecies of conftitution, is the general will; and it muft be the determination of

political conftitutions to youth, which they might not obtain by perufing differtations. He has feen copies of the Diagrams, prepared for the printfhops, with poetic and familiar explanations, intended to diffufe this fpecies of knowledge among the people, and inftruct them to difcern the deceitful, often fraudulent, conduct of their pretended reprefentatives.

A Bookfeller has conveyed to the Author the following Letter, which contains a better critique on the pamphlet than will probably be given in any other manner:

"SIR,

YOUR mode of illuftrating political problems by Diagrams is a valuable and important difcovery; and if you had confined your abilities to them and their explanations, you would have fixed your name among fcientific and permanent benefactors of the world: but you have difdained to write an elementary book, where elements are unknown, and fo much wanted, and you have indulged fatire, which, however juft, is unworthy of you, and will be more advantageous to the bookfeller than to you.

I am, &c."

the general will, that every citizen, without distinction of birth, possessions, or talents, enjoy the great objects of society—liberty, property, and security.

Liberty is a power, obtained for every citizen by the disposition and engagement of the general force, to act for his own happiness, without injuring others: and all beyond it, is licence.

The right of property, does not relate merely to the tenement or land which forms may convey, but to the necessary justice, that men of every condition should enjoy the advantages of their honest industry, and not be obliged to sacrifice them to the pride and pleasure of others:

And social security, arises from the engagement of the whole community to preserve the person, property, and liberty of every individual, untouched while unoffending.

That the general will may be expressed, without assembling the nation, or investing the people with the executive power — which is the vulgar idea of Democracy—is not only rendered probable, but demonstrated, by the diagram of the Constitution of Alfred. For though the Mycle-gemot was called the Folk-mot; and every freeman might attend who
found

found subject of complaint in any act of government, the Mycle-gemot was not a part of government: it enacted no laws, but such as were constitutional; it performed no office of the executive power, but adjudged it; and the assembly of the National Deputies was never too numerous for deliberation.

The English House of Lords is a remnant of that Assembly; and its claims of judging, in dernier resort, &c. are derived from it. But the House of Lords was sunk, by the regulations of William the Conqueror, into a branch of the ordinary government; the ministers or managers of which, in all departments, assiduously discredit every mode of expressing the general will: being sensible, the numerous abuses which render their situations lucrative, would be abolished, and that no measures could obtain its sanction, not favourable to the general interest.

The National Assembly, having assumed powers similar to those of the Mycle-gemot, I rejoiced in the hope that France would furnish the example of a society organised into a political body, to which the head and the limbs would be vitally annexed;

which would be actuated by a common principle of intereſt, by a common reaſon, judgment, and will: and that England, ſtimulated by generous emulation, might be induced to reviſe its government, correct its errors, and remove its inconveniencies.

I entertained theſe hopes, without the proſpect of any advantage to myſelf, my ſon, my brother, or my couſin, but in common with all my fellow citizens; without eſtimating the injuries that might enſue, to thoſe orders which had privileges by inheritance, thoſe prieſts who were creeping up the tortuous paths of ſervile ambition, or thoſe ſplendid adventurers who had talked and written credulous multitudes into an opinion that the general induſtry muſt be deeply taxed to gratify and ſupport them.

But your Royal Highneſs will conceive my ſituation and feel for me, when the voice of Burke, like that of the angel in the fiery cloud, entranced my faculties, and wholly changed the direction of my imagination.

Farewel Reaſon—Science—Truth—all ideas of thoſe rights, or of that juſtice, claimed for all mankind by a ſoft and whimpering philoſophy! Welcome, conſecrated Deſpotiſm—whether cloathed in

the

the dreadful armor of Kings, the soft lawn of Bishops, or the various garbs of Senators, Magistrates, Lawyers, Orators, Parasites, Panders, or Pimps. From thy caprices are derived law, the security of property, the patronage of talents, the encouragement of industry; and from thy authority or command arise independence and liberty.

By this new information or new light, I mean to conduct your Royal Highness through the elaborate, intricate, and mystic production of Mr. Edmund Burke; as through a luxuriant wilderness, where tyranny, privilege, superstition, and intolerance, display their magic rites, and combine, with their own, the supposed interests of heaven and hell.

As the industrious mechanic, whose fancy has been limited by the horizon of his humble state; on looking into the divine compositions of the northern prophet, loses his common faculties, and deigns to converse only with spirits—so it befel me, having perused the unparalleled work of the political Swedenbourg, I, no longer, traced principles from facts, or sought truth in the long, the cautious, the laborious processes of demonstration: I saw the dreadful precipices of Atheism terminating all the paths of science: and I 'piously' funk into the bosom of intuitive credulity, where I found, all truths on heavenly authorities; riches, ranks, and distinctions, without the requisitions of merit; the happiness of human nature, at the will of the fortunate; and nations, as herds of cattle, transmitted by inheritance. How grateful, this state of things, to the indolence, the selfishness, and the love of power, so easily excited in the human mind!—You will not wonder, I quitted the simple paths of inquiry and investigation, for those enchanted labyrinths into which political mysticism conducted me.

Your Royal Highness is particularly requested to observe, the admirable address, with which this great writer introduces the subject of his work.

It is frequently the misfortune of societies or clubs in London, to have less prudence than good intention.

In the use of those rites of 'pious' magic, which are thought to engage the Deity even in the most sordid offices of human life, a club, calling itself the Revolution Society, employed a nonconformist clergyman as its magician: and he solemnly invoked his God, on a festival destined to another purpose, in

behalf

behalf of those " levelling furies" in France, who, in demolishing the ancient and " sacred" temple of absolute monarchy, nearly buried the king, the queen, the nobility, and the clergy, in the ruin.

But the magician does not worship the God of the country.* He is therefore liable to the charge of atheism, as I shall presently demonstrate to your Royal Highness: his incantations are impieties; and, if the true spirit of Mr. Burke's religion could have its proper effect, he would be soon silenced by the 'holy' severities of the inquisition. This circumstance alone, would invalidate his positions; and render null, the resolutions and proceedings of a society, of which he affects to be the Pontiff.

But, in the luxuriance of our author's sublime generosity, and in the ebullitions of 'holy' zeal, he condescends to consider his principles and to confute his arguments: and your Royal Highness will see, with pleasing exultation, this " incomparable" orator proves, on the authority of the Revolution—that the English cannot elect their kings; cannot cashier them for misconduct; or form a government for themselves.

* Price is a professed Arian.

Your

Your Royal Highness will admire his manner of passing over or expunging every idea of election in the appointment of William the Third, though he was actually chosen King, and the Crown made hereditary in his family by the Queen.

His dexterity must be deemed important and astonishing, when he transmutes the delicacy of the convention, in the use of the word Abdication, into a proof that if James had not fled, the nation in arms, assisted by the Prince of Orange, could not have dethroned him, without incurring the guilt of treason.

Here the doctrine of Hobbes is insinuated with all the art of the author's eloquence: but he does not refer to the Leviathan; for Hobbes was an Atheist. Your Royal Highness must perceive another privilege of mystic piety. No instruments, in earth or hell, are forbidden to a Saint, if conducive to his interest. Fiends are not so horrible to our author as Atheists. But as the Devil is said to believe or to have faith, Mr. Hobbes, though an Atheist, coinciding with the orthodoxy of Mr. Burke in the creed of Absolute Monarchy, his sentiments may be adopted without contaminating the author's soul, or sullying his 'righteous' reputation. But it was highly prudent

dent, not to mention Hobbes; and gratitude is not among the obligations of myſticiſm.

Such the author deems to be the depraved condition of Europe, from Philoſophy and Atheiſm, that if he had derived Royalty directly from Heaven, he might have been embarraſſed by heralds and genealogiſts; he therefore mingles and jumbles the ſubjects of government, hereditary monarchy, and myſtic religion. This is done, with wonderful art and deſign.—The Sceptic, Philoſopher, Patriot, or Atheiſt — all ſynonimous terms — is accuſtomed to view and examine all contrivances in their principles, and all compoſitions in their elements. The united ſkill and penetration of Europe, could not analyſe, without completely diſſipating, the work before us. It ſeems, ſometimes air, ſometimes fire: it aſſumes fantaſtic ſhapes, which vary in every point of view, and will not bear the touch of impertinent and profane philoſophy.

I exerciſe the privilege of the initiated, when I preſume to aſſiſt your Royal Highneſs in contemplating this wonderful fabric.

Mr. Burke has given his " unparalleled " work all the properties and effects of a *Camera Obſcura,* or of a magic

magic lanthorn. Government and Royalty are displayed, not as arising from the mud and filth of popular interposition; but descending from Heaven, at the command of Religion, which waves her wand from a turret of the Inquisition, and awes the nations into implicit faith and unconditioned loyalty.—Kings and Queens are glorious suns and chaste moons. The beauty of holiness, is exhibited in all the gradations of the Hierarchy; the Pope being slightly veiled. The varied effects of noble birth, exalted rank, knight-errantry and chivalry—all the fruits of all the virtues—are charmingly engrafted on all the vices; while the multitude, is irretrievably and eternally fixed to the earth, and forms the immeasurable pavement supporting the privileged and consecrated scene!

What would be, the demonstrations of a Newton, to the consequences of such a spectacle, on the majorities of all nations!—Who would turn an eye, to the natural, unornamented delineations, of Mathematicians, Economistes,* Patriots, and Atheists!

Hail,

* The author has been criticised for censuring Economists, while his regulations in the Royal Kitchen are splendid proofs of his own love of Economy. But, the Economistes of France are political, and they are associated, not to inspect sauce-

Hail, heavenly Enthusiasm! parent of mystic despotism and arbitrary power.—How sublime thy ordinances; how captivating thy arrangements, compared with the cold tenets of Philosophy, and the groveling principles of Patriotism!

Having given Kings, Queens, Nobles, and High-Priests, a heavenly origin, without directly asserting it—and having by consecration rendered them unassailable—he rises into a strain of sublime scurrility against the National Assembly—for violences to which they were not accessary, and some of which never existed except in his own imagination. But the purpose justifies the means. The King of France, is the Sun shorn of his beams; the Queen is the Morning Star precipitated from her orbit: and the authors of their degradation, are not entitled to the exceptions of truth, on that principle of religion, which keeps no faith with heretics.

sauce-pans, mops, and dish-clouts, but to produce and collect such facts and experiments, as may furnish Principles of Political Economy. Dr. Smith, the author of the History of the Wealth of Nations, derived the principal materials of his excellent work from this Society. But as their labours have not a tendency to promote Popery, the Ecclesiastics, particularly the Monks, brand them as Atheists; and our author, in holy reprehensions, and infamous imputations, closely imitates the glowing language of the Monks.

It

. It is true, the National Assembly, the Economistes, the Patriots, and the Atheists of France, were as little concerned in the violences at Versailles, in the humiliating procession of the King and Queen, and in their confinement to the Louvre, as the most enlightened and virtuous citizens of England in the riot and conflagration of 1780. The principal instigators and agents were truly catholic fish-women; as orthodox, as prejudiced, and almost as bigotted as our author. But in holy crimination— as in love and war—all advantages are to be seized, and all means are justifiable.—In the descriptions of the condition of France; of a general absence of all government, all law, and all order——of bloody Democrats, seeking the sacred remnants of an 'honourable' Nobility and 'holy' Clergy, and murthering them in multitudes: in these descriptions, the author avails himself of the justifiable licence of an orator; and almost every page of the declamation contains a misrepresentation, or an untruth. Besides, Mr. Burke is supported by the aristocratic newspapers of France and England; and this, in any case, is sufficient ground for that species of oratory we call Billingsgate.

Besides,

Your Royal Highness will observe, without contrast, the display of royalty would have no effect. The fall of the Queen, like that of a star, should be at the incantation of the dæmon of patriotism issuing from a charnel house; at every step, murthering millions, and his path a river of human blood. If I might presume to blame an author of such exalted abilities, I would say Mr. Burke has been squeamish, timid, too attentive to probability, and has not given sufficient scope to his creative imagination in his atrocious description of France.

Your Royal Highness will consider this observation as an answer to those little critics; who have cavilled at his description of the Queen, as defective *in costume*; contradicting popular ideas of character and manners, and indicating impiety; for it is a plagiarism from an office to the holy Virgin, adored as the morning star appearing on the horizon, and promising a heavenly day, &c. But minutiæ are unworthy a great genius; and the history of canonizations abounds with examples of a similar nature.

St. Grill, Bishop of Alexandria, assassinated the beautiful and sublime Hypathia; yet was canonized.

The hands of Charlemagne were loathſome with the blood of the Saxons, whom he maſſacred without the pretence of juſtice: he robbed his nephews of their patrimony; married four wives, yet committed inceſt: but he increaſed the territory of the church, and the church made him a Saint. In another edition, I hope the author will paint him at length; give him the attributes of an evening ſtar; and place him as a companion to the moſt brilliant production of his pencil.

Having thrown a luſtre on his doctrines concerning royalty; which will more rapidly promote their circulation than a demonſtration of their truth—and having harrowed up, at leaſt his own ſoul, on the impiety, the ſacrilege, and the villainy, of degrading and limiting its prerogatives in France—he denies the right of the people, to form or model a government; for a reaſon, which muſt be convincing to every man of equal piety with the author—that Government is an Inſtitution of God; tranſmitted from one generation to another, in all its forms and privileges. In this matter, he acts as gamblers do at play—by guarding againſt poſſible chances. He uſes the phraſe " Government is a
" human

"human Invention:" but denies the neceffity of general approbation or general will. He places religion as the bafis of fociety: and if religion be a hum, an invention, it is that of priefts, who are the inftruments of the Divinity, and fpeak his will. Thus an apparent contradiction may be explained; as in this manner, government may be at the fame time the inftitution of God and the invention of man.

I was the more embarraffed on this part of the fubject, as I had been long accuftomed to think, the virtues of men had no dependence on their mode of worfhipping God; that the opinion had been propagated by political hypocrites, who enforced without believing it; and had been adopted by the common people in circumftances fo depreffed that they thought themfelves obliged to believe without examination, whatever was enjoined them.

On a general view of hiftory, by reafon alone, the profperity of nations had appeared to me, to depend only on the excellence of their government and legiflation.

The Jews were eminently pure in their worfhip; and the Egyptians and Perfians to them were Atheifts

ists—The morals of the latter were good; those of the former abominable.

Rome, when it produced the virtues of Decius and Fabricius, was Pagan and atheistic: Constantinople was the reservoir of all the most detestable vices, after Constantine had introduced the Christian religion.

We have Apostolic, Catholic, and most Christian Kings; but no Titus, no Trajan, no Antoninus.

The Italians, the Spaniards, the Portuguese, have more religion than all Europe: but are their morals proportionably distinguished? What Christian would compare ancient and modern Greece, or ancient and modern Rome, in respect to religion; what philosopher would compare them, in respect to talents, industry, or merit?

My reason therefore concluded that religion was not virtue.

Why, I have exclaimed with regret and anguish, are priests suffered to light up the torch of intolerance, to strew kingdoms with the famished or mangled carcases of those honest inhabitants who would have cultivated them; if the goodness of man in society be wholly the effect of the laws? I therefore earnestly

nestly wished, that governments might have the wisdom to permit religion privately to regulate the faith of individuals; and that manners and virtues might be wholly consigned to the laws.

My presumptuous philosophy proceeded farther. The government of priests, as in Jerusalem, in modern Rome, in Madrid, in Lisbon, &c. has always debased the nations which have submitted to it.

Under every form of religion, I concluded, man must become wicked, if his interest be detached from the public: if he cannot procure his own happiness but by the misery of others; and if the government neglect virtue, reward vice, or elevate it to honors and opulence.

Your Royal Highness will therefore imagine my pleasure, when all these conclusions of reason and all the anguish with which they had induced me to view the principles and proceedings of modern governments—were dissipated by a heavenly ray from the mystic genius of our political Swedenbourg.

He has taught me, that nations are " corporate " bodies" by consecrated charters from heaven: and that my concern for the condition or qualities of the people,

people, has been fanciful and superfluous; for their happiness is not the object of the present dispensations of Providence. They are irrevocably predestined to a state of perpetual labor and industry; the best produce of which is to ascend for the use and gratification of higher orders and classes, which are entitled by " sacred" claims to the various privileges of the mysterious corporations.

I wondered no longer, at the glowing epithets of reproach, execration, and horror, with which our " pious" author, reprobated the National Assembly of France, for demolishing an ancient government, the institution of the Deity, and degrading royal, noble, sacred, and privileged ranks, in favour of wretched, savage animals, called the people; just emerged from mere brutality; and, to be disciplined, under the direction of their masters, by labor and misery here, for corporate privileges hereafter.

But the patriotism of this great man, is superior even to his benevolence. The possibility that the destructive dæmon of prophane philosophy, may be wafted over to England, has distracted him almost into insanity; and his spirit often flies to the cliffs of
Dover,

Dover, waving that of his " immortal" work in the form of a flaming fword, and guarding the " in- " comparable ftructure of the Englifh Conftitu- " tion," from the impious affaults of democratic atheifts and infernal furies. Befides, the good man has been thirty years, climbing its lofty towers, and dragging up the knights of his family for its defence.

This patriotifm induces him, at intervals, to give fublime and myftic hints concerning the origin and formation of that Conftitution. We are to be content with hints, until the enormities of the times be fub- fided, and he may be at leifure to afcend that region of the feven heavens, where the records of earthly cor- porations are preferved.* If I live to the æra of his afcenfion—have more leifure from indifpenfable en- gagements, and more refpite from the pains and in- firmities of age—I fhall not, as I now do, throw rockets to light him on his way: but I will patiently furvey the full effect of his miffion; and ferioufly

* It was, in an excurfion to that region, he difcovered the neceffity of deftroying the charter of the Eaft India Company; and in confequence of the difcovery, furnifhed the heads of Mr. Fox's India Bill; the rejection of which lies as a fin on the nation.

examine the records he produces, by the beſt abilities that remain with me.

In the mean time, I cannot help expreſſing my aſtoniſhment, that he has only obſcurely hinted the origin of our government, and has not deſcribed it with that frantic eloquence, which every man of learning and taſte, on the peruſal of the work before us—muſt pronounce "unparalleled" in all the productions of ancient and modern literature.

An opinion is never ſo effectually impreſſed on the public, as when accompanied by terror and aſtoniſhment. I cannot imagine a reaſon, that a writer of Mr. Burke's talents and principles, ſhould have omitted an occaſion ſo ſplendid, as is offered, by the God of the country * deſcending in flaming clouds on Snowden or Skiddow, and giving into the bloody hands of the "pious" and intrepid conqueror, the permanent conſtitution and everlaſting inheritance of the land. Here the diadem of deſpotiſm is held, as it ought to be, by the vicar of God on earth. While the iſland is ſtrewed with the dead and dying, it is divided among chiefs whom avarice and a ſpirit of rapine induced to accompany their leader; and

* This phraſe will ſoon be explained.

the

the grandeur of the church and the dignity of its miniſters are provided for, by eſtates wreſted from the wretched inhabitants.

No ſubject can eſcape cavil. All the kingdom was in effect confiſcated; and all rights ſunk before the regulations of that revolution: but every thing was ſanctioned, not as in France at this time, by views of public relief and the benefit of all the people, but by the power of the ſword conſecrated by God's Vicar on Earth.

This is the origin of the conſtitution, for which our author ſo violently contends: and here the rights of royalty, nobility, and the church, received that ſacred character, that perpetual inviolability, which render all attempts at reform or innovation—treaſon and ſacrilege.

The author, with commendable prudence, avoids cenſuring the Reformation with ſeverity—as intereſts and prejudices having been created by it, too numerous to be oppoſed. But he approaches it circuitouſly, and brands with infamy the horrible ſacrilege of the eighth Henry in deſpoiling the church of its PROPERTY.

Whether

Whether it be practicable to remove the guilt of that transaction, "which presses heavily on the land," I will not determine. The present administration has been merciful, to the descendants of men who had incurred forfeitures by rebellion. If Mr. Burke should be restored to power—and it must be the wish of every " pious" man he may—the least to be expected from his fervid zeal, is a complete restoration of the PROPERTY of the church.

But waving this 'seductive' hope, I must observe to your Royal Highness, that the 'sacred' privileges and rights lately violated in France, have a similar origin to those of England, and were repeatedly sanctioned by God's Vicar on Earth.

In England, several events have gradually encroached on them. The reformation had some effect: but the wound inflicted would have been soon healed, if the " diabolical" art of printing had not been invented. That diffused knowledge into classes destined to be ignorant; forced literature out of the regulating hands of the clergy; and produced those enemies to all fixed institutions, those parents of impertinent inquiry, investigation, discussion, knowledge,

ledge, and science, the literati,* the free-thinkers, and the philosophers.

These " Atheists"—for, after the example of my author, I shall compress them into one odious denomination. These " Atheists" have waged perpetual war with privileges, institutions, and prejudices— and your Royal Highness will shudder, when informed, they have nearly obtained a power, the most fatal to all " sacred" pretensions—" the legal " Liberty of the Press."†

* The best scholar of this country, in the usual sense of the word, and one of its best men, died in the house of a Sheriff's Officer. This affecting event gave rise to the Society for the establishment of a Literary Fund. Mr. Burke was requested to assist in the institution; but he treated the application with such angry rudeness, and with such abuse of literature, that the gentleman who conveyed the message of the Society thought him insane. No---said one of his political friends---but he hates every man who would participate with him, the smallest portion of literary fame.

† Mr. Burke has greatly consoled the 'pious' votaries of ancient order and privilege, by announcing the conversion of Newgate into a Bastille. The punishment of Lord George Gordon has been generally thought too severe, while Mr. and Madame la Motte distributed volumes with impunity on the same subject. Public disapprobation would have ensued, if Lord George had not been peculiarly unpopular. It was not however imagined, until Mr. Burke disclosed the secret, that future informations ex officio, where families and privileges are concerned, may serve the purposes of Lettres de Cachet.

Another

Another principle of innovation, on the constitution of the conqueror—was produced by the "incautious" introduction and imprudent encouragement of industry.

The beautiful order of those provisions, made by William, for a strong, effective government, must have often struck the imagination of your Royal Highness. The division of the kingdom into sixty thousand portions, or in effect into so many properties—the summary mode of disposing of the common people, and excluding them from all political questions—the "complete representation" of the country "in "masses" by the chiefs of those divisions; and above all, the sanction and co-operation of an opulent clergy, firmly pledged to preserve the people in implicit obedience and perpetual labor by the hopes of future rewards: those arrangements formed a constitution, which is considered by our author, as an inheritance, for the defence of which, Englishmen should shed the last drop of their blood.

Human ingenuity, however, devised means to elude a power it could not resist. Small settlements at the mouths of rivers produced mechanics and artists, who could not be induced to exert their talents, at the command of the King, the Barons, the Clergy, or in any mode but by obtaining an equivalent. Thus sprung up industry and trade—mortal enemies to privilege and arbitrary power.

Finding these new guests convenient to the revenue, princes ' imprudently' encouraged them—until general opinion was diffused, that ingenuity and industry should not be exerted by the people, without obtaining an equivalent.

To favor the progress of that opinion, alienations of fiefs were allowed—lands were thrown into circulation—trade and commerce were established—new orders were generated: and that system of political œconomy was imagined, which produced numerous innovations * in England; and had some effect in France, besides forming that society called ECONOMISTES; the peculiar objects of our author's abhorrence.

Mr. Burke says, he cannot distinctly enumerate the crimes and enormities which must have called down the vengeance of heaven on the monarchy of France,

* The House of Commons, the Habeas Corpus Act, the Revolution, &c. &c.

and

and which, he seems to think, may affect that of England.

It would be "impious" to imagine that any errors of royalty, of the nobility or clergy—and those sacred orders are incapable of crimes—should have effects so opposite to what our author affects to know to be the will of "heaven."

The causes certainly are—the partial liberty of the press—the introduction of the ideas of necessary equivalents for all services—and the encouragement of industry, trade, and commerce.

The society called Economistes, in correspondence with ingenious men in every State of Europe, adopted these causes as principles—and they contributed considerably to all the late improvements in agriculture, in the useful arts; and particularly to the diffusion and encouragement of the opinion, that industry is intitled to an equivalent from those who enjoy its effects, and that government should treat it as property, to be taxed only by the consent of its possessors.

This opinion has emancipated from feodal vassalage those portions of the people, who enjoy civil or political liberty. And if it be examined, only by reason,

son, it will prove demonstratively true. For if the Barons and Knights who received feodal possessions, contributed to the public service on consultation or by consent—every man who emerged from villainage and exercised his talents for an equivalent, became a free citizen, and could not reasonably or justly be taxed without his consent.

The difficulty of giving that consent without confusion, produced various efforts towards representation; which I shall not consider at this time. It is sufficient, that industry is the parent of modern liberty, and constitutes a claim to it, at least as indisputable as the possession of land or the will of a conqueror, or the bull of a Pope.

As industry took place of villainage and every species of servile dependence on the King, the Nobility, and the Clergy—nations urged their claims to be considered and consulted in all the important occurrences of government.

Here is the foundation of reproach and execration against the philosophical and political Economistes. The people would have acquired the rights of citizens, and the constitutional power of chusing their masters and governors, without understanding or exerting

exerting them—if these philosophers had not urged them to their duties, often with hazard and injury, from the oppressors and the oppressed.

Plans for the improvement of agriculture, and for the direction of genius and ingenuity into all the useful arts, were formed and promoted by the Economistes throughout Europe; and the names of all the real benefactors of human nature, in the late progress of civil improvements, are to be found in their societies or among their correspondents.— But they proceeded in a direction, opposite to that of all feodal institutions:—all their efforts were intended to elevate the people, and by destroying the enormous inequalities which blended barbarous splendor with loathsome misery, and the most unbounded licence with the most abject slavery.

But this does not constitute their principal offence. The Economistes; enthusiasts in the contemplation of nature; and, of all men, the most sincere adorers of the ineffable principle which actuates it—abhorred the monks, for their ignorance, impositions, and vices; and mere negligence of a malignant monk, ensures the imputation of atheism.

If

If it be true, that ' none by searching can find ' out God'—every man on earth is an Atheist. If difference of opinion concerning the Deity, be a ground of imputation; the Trinitarian must be an Atheist to the Arian, and the Socinian to both: the Mahometan to the Christian; the Christian to the Jew; the Jew to the Hindu; the Hindu to the Chinese, &c. &c. for they do not worship the same gods: and the deities of modern religions do not recognise and acknowledge each other.

It is thus in fact—all men are Atheists, in the estimation of particular sects, except the members of those sects: and they are Atheists, to the rest of the world.

This occasion of discord, ill-will, and hatred, is of advantage, only to the priests of the innumerable sects, that divide the world.

But your Royal Highness will admire the address and oratorical art of our great author, who employs the most odious epithet in all the languages of Europe, to discredit the principal authors of the French Revolution. If he had played on them, the engines that have annoyed the political party, in which he is embarked: if he had said, of them, what the Public strongly

strongly affirm of all the members of the ENGLISH COALITION, that all their plans and measures are directed to their immediate or remote advantage: every movement in the French Revolution would have demonstrated the falsehood. No arrangements, in the history of mankind, have been made, with views so disinterested and so generous. All power, gradually arises from the people, and by election. The elected hold their places for very moderate advantages and for short periods, and are incapacitated for office during a considerable interval. This is, probably, a measure of wisdom: it is, certainly, a proof of disinterestedness and generosity.

But whither am I straying? Have the charms of philosophy again fascinated me? Our Author has pronounced the Economistes Atheists, with the views of a brutal boy, who consigns a dog to destruction, by calling him mad. But your Royal Highness will not wonder at this charge, when you understand, the first measure suggested by these votaries of impiety was the sacrilegious seizure of Ecclesiastical PROPERTY.

In England, this is a new idea; but, in the Author's opinion, we are but Semi-Christians. We

con-

consider benefices, tithes, &c. as appropriated to certain uses, and consigned to a certain order in trust, but not in right, and not as property. No doubt is here entertained, that Parliament may regulate, control, and correct the abuses of such a trust, and even change the uses of its funds, when detrimental to the Public.

A learned prelate, by no means insensible to the dignity, or uninformed in the rights of his order, has solicited his metropolitan to obtain a law, that would affect the Constitution, and dispose of the riches of the church.

But in the church of Rome, and in the opinion of Mr. Burke, trust and right are confounded. Whatever may be alledged on the destination of tithes—whatever frauds and villainies have been practised to accumulate ecclesiastical riches: being appropriated to the altar, they are sacred, and the application of them to national purposes, is robbery and sacrilege.

Your Royal Highness should also be informed, that some young men of this school, have lately derided the Roman Catholic religion—and proposed various means of introducing a popular system of morality.

To juſtify the invectives of our author, I will produce A Creed, which they attempted to ſubſtitute for that of St. Athanaſius; and they wiſhed the Biſhop D'Autun to pronounce it, at the grand feſtival of the National Federation.

I need not deſcribe to your Royal Highneſs, the proceedings of that Federation. The Biſhop D'Autun, attended by a large body of Clergy, performed the ſervice called High Maſs at the altar; and wherever a creed was to be introduced, the youthful Economiſtes propoſed the following:

Biſhop D'Autun (looking at the Clergy)——

" No longer, a confederation againſt the public—no longer devouring the harveſts and fruits, like the graſshoppers of Egypt—we, the miniſters of a religion which is truly catholic, conſign our minds and hearts to the glorious objects of a free conſtitution——and this—we ſwear——

CATHOLIC CREED.

" We believe—that God created man—to be the friend, not the oppreſſor of man——that he has given him fenſibility, memory, and reaſon.

It is the will of God, that human reaſon, rouſed by want, and inſtructed by experience, ſhall provide

our

our fuftenance, fhall lead us to cultivate the earth, invent and improve the inftruments of labor, and perfect all the fciences of real neceffity.

It is the will of God—that by gradually cultivating the fame reafon, not by fubmitting to the dogmas of others, all men fhould difcover and practife the focial duties, the means of maintaining order, and the knowledge of the beft legiflation.

This, being the whole of the will of God, and implying every thing neceffary to the formation of a good citizen, we hope the motives to merit, either in heaven or earth, the rewards of genius and activity, will never more be fought in trifling operations, praying, fafting, hair-cloth, and felf-caftigation, which have not the merit of leaping, dancing, and walking on the rope.

" The throne of the monarch of the univerfe, fhall no more be furrounded by faints; enemies to fociety, and the gloomy adverfaries of human happinefs. We fhall celebrate only the benefactors of mankind, Lycurgus, Solon, Brutus, Sydney; the inventors of ufeful arts, or of fome pleafure conformable to the general intereft.

"No moral inſtruction ſhall have authority in the ſtate, but ſuch as is ſanctioned by a ſenate, the real and unequivocal repreſentation of the whole people. It is from ſuch a body only, a beneficent government can be expected; perfectly tolerant, not expenſive, offering no ideas of the Divinity but ſuch as are grand, ſolemn, or amiable; exciting in the human mind the love of talents and virtue; and having no object but the happineſs of the people.

"The magiſtrates of the nation, being ſucceſſively appointed, and frequently inſtructed by the public will, muſt gradually become ſagacious and juſt; and will be cloathed with temporal and ſpiritual powers; all contradiction between religion, morality, and patriotiſm will diſappear; all the people, after temporary diviſions and differences, will have the ſame principles, and the ſame idea of the ſcience of morals, in which it is important that all of them ſhould be equally inſtructed. *Amen.*"

Mr. Burke, on reading a compoſition ſo unornamented, ſo ſimple; referring to objects ſo groveling as Morality and the Public Good; and recollecting the myſtic ſublimity and ſupernatural language of the divine Athanaſius; would throw from him the
Econo-

Economiſtic Creed with unutterable ſcorn; and accelerate the volubility of his expreſſions, in execrating Philoſophical Impiety, which would ſubſtitute Reaſon for Religion, and diveſt human life of the conſolations of myſtery and ſuperſtition.

Is it wonderful, therefore, he has taken large draughts of the fiery ſpirit produced by his own infernal alembic—and in the paroxyſms of holy fury, applied every infamous and horrible epithet in the Engliſh language, to thoſe ſacrilegious robbers, and traiterous innovators, the Philoſophers and Economiſtes of France?

Having exhauſted his ſtrength, in this dreadful manner—at the concluſion of the work, he leads the reader, wearied and terrified, to conſider the ſtructure of the French conſtitution and the condition of the French finances.

By this artifice, he enſures the reader's diſguſt, at the delineation of organic arrangements, where the author is ſometimes miſtaken; ſometimes miſrepreſents; and always animadverts with unequivocal expreſſions of hatred.

The obſervations on the Paper-Money of the National Aſſembly, are alſo the ebullitions of mere zeal.

zeal. The subject of Money is as well understood in France as in England. The mode of issuing the Assignats, is the offspring of necessity, not of ignorance: and I have some apprehensions for the reason of our author, when his prophecies, concerning the future condition of France, are compared with events that may soon burst on his view.

But let us hope ' better' things.—So wonderful a portion of the spirit of prophecy, could not have been given in vain. If we may have faith, ' to remove ' mountains'—why not, to coincide with the pious Apostle of Despotism, in all his wishes and expectations?

His ' matchless' eloquence may induce all the Powers of Europe to unite——to publish a crusade against Philosophy, Free-thinking, and Democratic Patriotism——to pour innumerable armies into the heart of France—to sacrifice the majority of the nation at the shrine of the deified Queen; to restore the Nobility and Clergy to their honours and riches; to rebuild the Bastile, and fill it to the summit of its towers with Jacobins* and Atheists;—and to recover

---

* The Jacobins are Patriots, inclined to constitutional Democracy, and formed into a Club The reader should bear in mind, that

cover the military, clerical, and ancient government of the country.

I have thus endeavoured to delineate the general purpose, and point out the excellences and beauties of this great work.

My survey of it has been hasty—my time being unfortunately engaged——and infirmities checking my ardour and activity. I trust, however, no parts of considerable importance, have been omitted; and that your Royal Highness will not be displeased at my humble efforts to save you some trouble in examining them.

The Sun has spots—and the Astronomer mentions them, without the imputation of impiety.——Your Royal Highness will believe, I mean not to detract from the author's fame, by producing some peculiari-

---

that by Democracy in France is meant, the power of election and controul in the people, not, as in Greece and Rome, the faculties of actual government. The author confounds these ideas. And the Patriotic Club being his aversion, he compares it to the ' Lords of Articles,' who prepared Bills for the ancient Government of Scotland. The Jacobins probably settle their mode of proceeding in the National Assembly at their Club: but they are ' Lords of Articles' only as the Assemblies at the Duke of Portland's, at Brookes's, at Cumberland House, or Mrs. F———t's, may be called ' Lords or Ladies of Articles.'

ties

ties of his style and composition, when I assure you, I think the eloquence, imagery, and phraseology of the work, admirably calculated to diffuse the principles of it among the 'great vulgar and the little'—and that no man since the death of the ' immortal,' Whitfield, could enter into competition with him in this species of composition.

But as your Royal Highness is young; and may not have much attended to the varieties of English style: and I have had the presumption to assume the tone of an instructor—I will submit the following passages, as proofs of the validity of general opinion and literary fame.

Bombast, substituted for Philosophy.

Page 68. " This preponderating weight being added to the force of the body chicane in the Tiers Etat, completed that momentum of ignorance, rashness, presumption, and lust of plunder, which nothing has been able to resist."

Vulgarity, to heighten admiration.

P. 71. " *It is a thing to be wondered at, to see how very soon France, when she had a moment to respire, reco-*

recovered and emerged from the longest and most dreadful civil war that ever was known."

A classic passage, disgraced by its accompaniments.

P. 86. " I have nothing to say to the clumsy subtilty of their political metaphysics. Let them be their amusement in the schools.—' Illa *se jactet in* ' *aula—Æolus, et clauso ventorum carcere regnet.*'—But let them not *break prison* to burst like a *Levanter*, to sweep the earth with their hurricane, and to *break up* the fountains of the great deep to overwhelm us."

A paradox, most convenient when a falsehood is to be covered or ignorance concealed.

P. 91. " The pretended rights of these theorists are all extremes; and in proportion as they are metaphysically true, they are morally and politically false."

Indelicate allusions, to assist the sale of the work.

P. 93. " I confess to you, Sir, I never liked this continual talk of resistance and revolution, or the practice of making the extreme medicine of the constitution its daily bread. It renders the habit of society

ciety dangerously valetudinary: it is taking periodical doses of mercury sublimate, and swallowing down repeated provocatives of cantharides to our love of liberty."

Borrowed from a taylor; and expressed correctly in his manner.

P. 104. "We are said to learn manners at second-hand from your side of the water, and that we dress our behaviour in the frippery of France. If so, we are still in the old cut."

This should have been harmonised by Sir Joshua Reynolds.

P. 108. "A groupe of regicide and sacrilegious slaughter, was indeed boldly sketched, but it was only sketched. It unhappily was left unfinished, in this great history-piece of the massacre of *innocents*. What hardy pencil of a great master, from the school of the rights of men, will finish it, is to be seen hereafter."

This will offend his countrymen, the common Irish, who

who resent any sarcastic reference to their fellow-creatures.

P. 117. " Happy if learning, not debauched by ambition, had been satisfied to continue the instructor, and not aspired to be the master! Along with its natural protectors and guardians, learning will be cast into the mire, and trodden down under the hoofs of a swinish multitude."

The paragraph being destined for the people, is designedly obscure, if not unintelligible. The CHURCH has declared, that Ignorance is the mother of Devotion.

P. 140. " When the people have emptied themselves of all the lust of selfish will, which without religion it is utterly impossible they ever should, when they are conscious that they exercise, and exercise perhaps in an higher link of the order of delegation, the power, which to be legitimate must be according to that eternal immutable law, in which will and reason are the same, they will be more careful how they place power in base and incapable hands."

How beautifully this is perplexed! The works of a prophet always require an interpreter.

P. 145. " Perfuaded that all things ought to be done with reference, and referring all to the point of reference to which all fhould be directed, they think themfelves bound, not only as individuals in the fanctuary of the heart, or as congregated in that perfonal capacity, to renew the memory of their high origin and caft."

Nafty, without occafion.

P. 151. " They are not repelled through a faftidious delicacy, at the ftench of their arrogance and prefumption, from a medicinal attention to their mental blotches and running fores."

To conftruct fentences of fcurrilous epithets; the author feems to have turned to the words ' Atheift,' Traitor and Robber, in Johnfon's Dictionary; and by the conjunction ' and,' to have connected them and all their fynonymes—when a Patriot or a Philofopher occurred to his imagination.

The work, on the whole, wants that lucid order, that

that air of demonſtration, which real ſcience gives to every ſpecies of argument.

The author's anger throughout, is not the emotion of a great and good mind: it is that of Milton's fiend contemplating the innocence of our firſt parents, and the poſſible happineſs of their race.

His imagery is incorrect, often diſtorted; and his language is rumbling, noiſy, and inharmonious.

But all myſtic productions ſhould have theſe " ſeeming" faults, to produce their effects on the multitude, who are always convinced if ſufficiently terrified; who are highly edified by unintelligible enigmas; and often adore a loquacious impoſtor, who by ſoothing their prejudices invades their rights; and on their credulity and miſery, erects his ſplendid fortune and his fame.

THE END.

This Day is published,

The THIRD EDITION, Price 2s. 6d. of

LETTERS ON POLITICAL LIBERTY, and the Principles of English and Irish Projects of Reform.

The first Edition of this Work was translated into French by M. LA FITE; the Translator was sent into the Bastile, the Translation burnt by the Executioner; but the Opinions of it had some Effect in the Appointment of Provincial Assemblies, and in the Efforts of the present Revolution; and its Principles *must* soon be adopted in England.

A SHORT REVIEW of the FRENCH REVOLUTION, in an ADDRESS from the NATIONAL ASSEMBLY to the People of France. Price 2s.

www.ingramcontent.com/pod-product-compliance
Lightning Source LLC
Chambersburg PA
CBHW020251170426
43202CB00008B/317